A i  k e s

Dedication

To the loving memory of my father,
who sadly passed away in 2013.

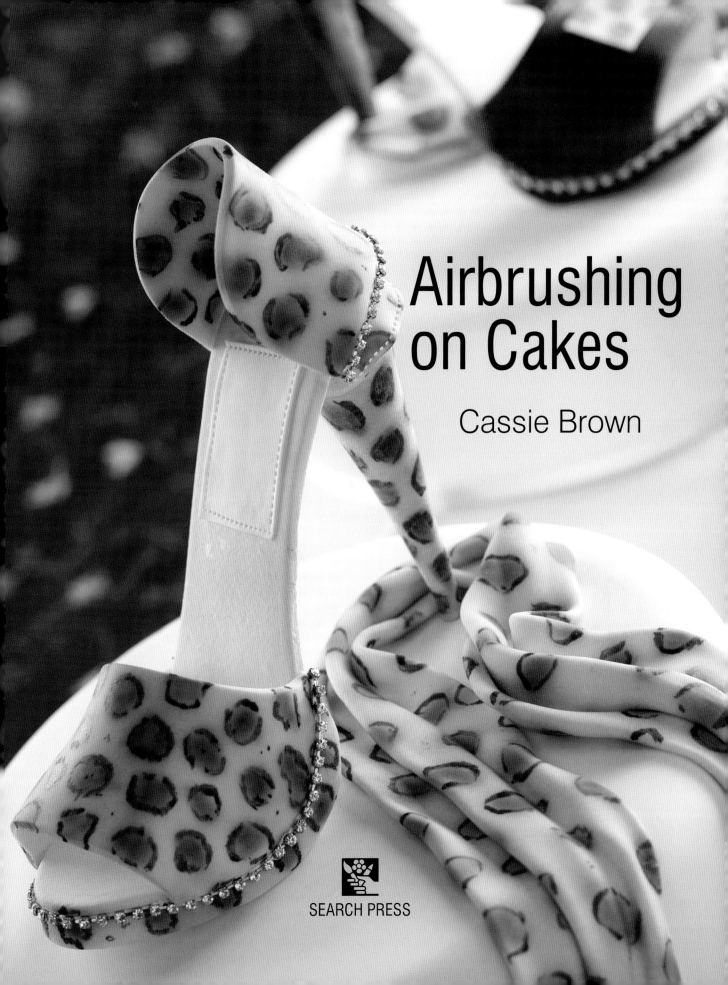

Airbrushing
on Cakes

Cassie Brown

SEARCH PRESS

First published in 2015

Search Press Limited
Wellwood, North Farm Road,
Tunbridge Wells, Kent TN2 3DR

Text copyright © Cassie Brown 2015

Photographs by Paul Bricknell at Search Press Studios,
except for page 10 (main image), by Maciej Galikowski at
Shesto Ltd.

Photographs and design copyright © Search Press Ltd 2015

ISBN: 978-1-78221-122-8

The Publishers and author can accept no responsibility for
any consequences arising from the information, advice or
instructions given in this publication.

Readers are permitted to reproduce any of the items in this
book for their personal use, or for the purposes of selling for
charity, free of charge and without the prior permission of the
Publishers. Any use of the items for commercial purposes is
not permitted without the prior permission of the Publishers.

Suppliers

If you have difficulty in obtaining any of the materials and
equipment mentioned in this book, then please visit the
Search Press website for details of suppliers:
www.searchpress.com

You are also invited to visit the author's website:
www.cassiebrown.com

Publisher's note

All the step-by-step photographs in this book feature the
author, Cassie Brown, demonstrating how to decorate cakes
using an airbrush. No models have been used.

Acknowledgements

I would like to thank Renshaw for supplying all the
sugarpaste and modelling paste used in this book;
Tracey Mann from Tracey's Cakes, for supplying the
lovely white chocolate modelling paste; and Shesto
for supplying the airbrushes and all of their support
and airbrushing knowledge.

Thank you to the photographer, Paul, who has
made my work look amazing and my editor,
Edward, for all the support, help and patience –
you've been fabulous. To all at Search Press for
being so friendly and welcoming at all times.

Thank you to Frances and Mike McNaughton for
being lovely hosts during the photoshoots.

Last of all, thank you to my husband Simon and my
three children, Charlotte, Sam and Harry, for all their
support at home.

Printed in China

CONTENTS

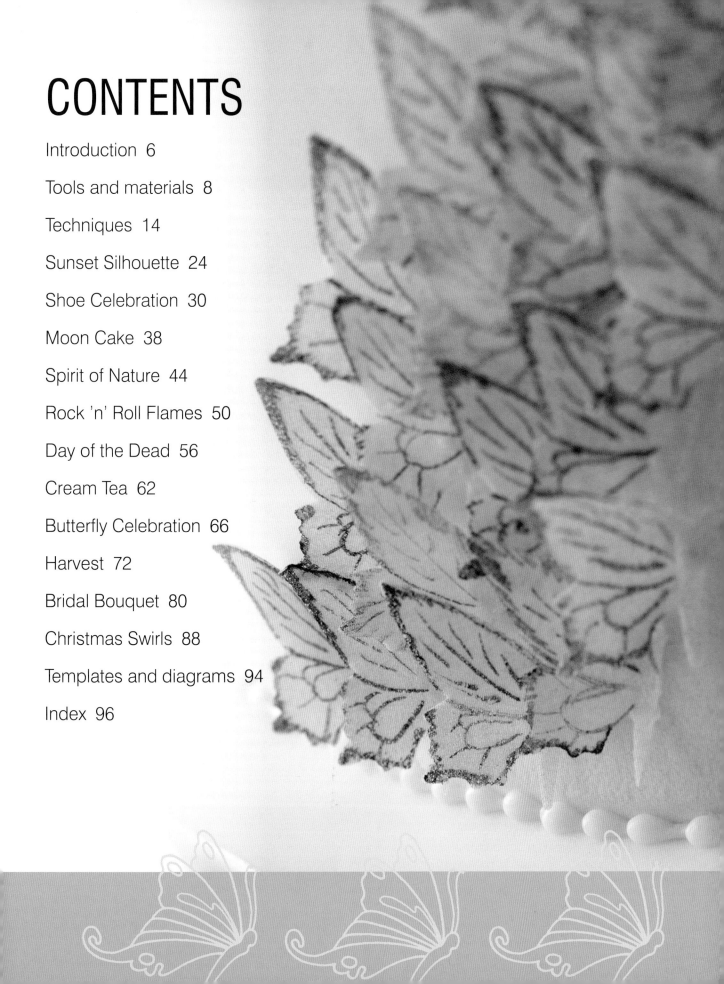

INTRODUCTION

When you were a child learning how to write and draw, you would take a crayon and scribble or doodle. Airbrushing is just the same. An airbrush is essentially a pen with edible ink flowing through it. You control the flow of ink by pulling back on the trigger. So, just as when you learned to write, using an airbrush is all about practice.

I wrote this book to ease you into airbrushing and show you what fabulous effects you can achieve. When I am at exhibitions or demonstrations, I always say that I don't need to sell the airbrush: it sells itself. The important bit of my job is to make you take the airbrush out of the box when you get home! Airbrushing will cut down on your work time as it is much quicker than other colouring methods.

However, this book is not just about using the airbrush to add block colours – it includes step-by-step instruction on carving and creating all the beautiful cakes in the book. From magically turning a sponge cake into a sugar pumpkin to creating delicate and beautiful chocolate roses, in this book I have shared it all with you.

Most of all, I hope the content of this book will take the fear factor out of airbrushing, and inspire you to push the boundaries of cake decorating – your airbrush can do so much more than just shading cakes.

TOOLS AND MATERIALS

This part of the book will tell you about recipes and the baking of the cakes including what tools you will need to cook the perfect cake.

Cake baking

It is very important that the cake tastes just as good as it looks, so always remember to get the foundations right before you start creating the decoration. My essential tools for baking are: 7.5cm (3in) deep cake tins in a variety of sizes and shapes, a cooling rack, cupcake tray and cupcake cases. You also need strong drum boards to support your cake from underneath and, optionally, thinner boards for presenting smaller cakes or if you want to experiment with tiers. 15mm (½in) wide ribbon is used to decorate the sides of the thick drum boards and help disguise gaps between stacked cakes. A turntable is also very useful as it allows you to smoothly rotate the cake when decorating without touching it.

Recipe

Cakes for decorating should have a firm but light texture. This recipe will carve well and taste great.

Mix 225g (8oz) butter together with the same amount of sugar until almost white and fluffy, then add two eggs. Mix together and gradually add 225g (8oz) self-raising flour along with another two eggs.

Line a tin fully with greaseproof paper, add the mixture and smooth over the top with the back of a spoon to get it evenly distributed in the tin. Place in a pre-heated oven for about twenty to thirty minutes at 140°C (280°F).

I take my sponge cakes out of the oven when they are just changing colour. If you gently press the top of the cake, it should bounce back. I leave the cake in the tin for ten minutes to settle before turning it out onto a cooling rack.

This recipe can be adapted for whatever size sponge cake I need. For a 31cm (12in) square cake, I would use 12oz (340g) of sugar, flour and butter along with six eggs. This will make a thin layer of sponge, but by cooking two or three of these you will get a good deep sponge cake. If you try to cook too much mixture in the tin, it will sink in the middle when baking in the oven.

Pastes and cake coverings

Pastes

The main covering for both cakes and boards in this book is **fondant** (sugarpaste); a fairly stiff material. After just a little kneading, fondant will roll out easily. The term can be confusing as 'fondant' can also be used to refer to watery icing that you would pour over small sponge cakes. In this book, it always refers to the rigid sugarpaste.

Modelling paste is similar to fondant (sugarpaste), though modelling paste is stiffer and stronger than fondant when dry. It can be bought from sugarcraft suppliers. It is used where decorative items are required to hold their shape, such as the stem of the pumpkin on page 75.

Flower paste, sometimes known as gum paste, is used for forming delicate sugar petals – hence the name. Similar to modelling paste, it is more elastic.

Buttercream

I make my own buttercream by adding icing sugar to softened butter, then adding a little vanilla essence. It is used as a filling for the scones in the Cream Tea project on pages 62–65.

Royal icing

A sweet, fluid mixture of egg whites and sugar, this sets hard and is used both as decoration and to help attach decorative pieces to cakes.

Jam/jelly

Used as a sweet, sticky filling, and also to help stick fondant (sugarpaste) to sponge.

Marzipan

A paste made from almonds and sugar, marzipan can be used as a layer between a fruit cake and an outer fondant (sugarpaste) covering. It can also be used as a modelling material and to fill small holes in cakes.

White modelling chocolate

A pliable chocolate paste that is used in this book for making white roses.

Fondant (sugarpaste), modelling paste and flower paste all have a similar appearance, but subtly different qualities.

Buttercream in a piping bag with a star nozzle.

Jam/jelly.

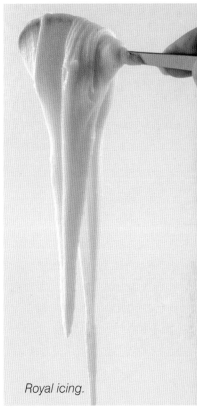

Royal icing.

Marzipan.

White modelling chocolate.

Airbrush

There are lots of different airbrushes on the market and they all work slightly differently, but the end results are very similar. Typically an airbrush has an air compressor, the airbrush itself and a hose to connect them. How the airbrush feels in your hand is very important as it needs to feel natural, so try to have a go with the airbrush you are looking at before buying. The biggest is not always the best for your cake decorating. If you have a very large compressor, turn down the flow of air – you do not want to blow your cake across the kitchen!

Airbrushes suitable for cake decorating have a colour well into which liquid food colours are added drop by drop. The well may be on top, or on the side.

Some airbrushes are single action, which means that there will be a constant flow of air and the colour will be released at a constant pressure from the airbrush. Other airbrushes are dual action, which allows you to control both the airflow and the colour coming through the nozzle. This gives you more control.

Whatever you eventually choose, it is well worth doing your research because once you start airbrushing, you will never look back. In fact, you will probably wonder how you coped without one.

Tip

Some airbrushes allow you to remove the protective nozzle cover to reveal the needle itself. This allows you some extra control for very fine lines and similar detail. This is not necessary for everyday airbrush use, but when you need extremely fine control, it is a useful trick to have up your sleeve. Be careful, as the needle itself is extremely fragile, and it is easy to lose the cover.

Colours

Airbrushes work with liquid edible food colours. Some are alcohol-based, and therefore not suitable for some religious or cultural restrictions. Powder dusts are available, but these can easily block your airbrush, so I recommend water-based colours. There are lots of different makes on the market, my favourite ranges being those with dropper nozzles which allow you great control. These dry almost instantly once sprayed onto the cake. Aside from the pink and violet, which may fade a little, all the colours are very strong and will not fade at all.

Multiple thin layers are better than single thick layers. If you spray too much colour onto your cake it will start to run down the cake, as the icing can only absorb so much colour at once. The secret is to gradually build the colour up in layers, so as soon as the cake starts to go shiny, stop and allow it to dry. If you are making a white cake black, for example, spray it a dark grey first then leave it for an hour or to before spraying a second layer to strengthen the tone to black.

The final colour can be affected by moisture in the atmosphere. Black can adopt a green tinge when applied in a humid room, and other colours can come out two or three shades darker. There is not a lot you can do about this, beyond buying a dehumidifer, or – more simply – waiting for a less humid day.

You can buy white airbrush colour for the airbrush but I personally do not use it, instead leaving the icing itself showing where I need white.

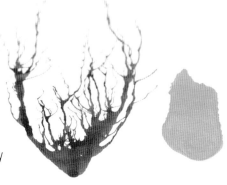

Tip

To check whether a certain colour will work through your airbrush, use this simple test: place a small drop of the colour directly onto a piece of paper. Holding the airbrush above the colour, use the airflow from your airbrush to blow the paint up the paper. If it splits into a 'scary tree' as on the left, it will be fine, but if it stays solid, or has any grains or lumps in it, as shown on the right, it may block your airbrush – avoid it.

Other tools and materials

Modelling tools I use food-grade metal dental tools which come in sets of three from craft or hardware stores. Each end is a slightly different shape, which makes them ideal for carving and moulding different shapes and textures.

Craft knife A small sharp-bladed knife is ideal for cutting small pieces of icing or cutting around templates.

Greaseproof paper This is used to make piping bags and line cake tins.

Small sieve or **tea strainer** You can push fondant (sugarpaste) though this to create textured grass.

Waterbrush When gently squeezed, a waterbrush will slowly release water which you can paint onto icing and use to secure decorations. I prefer to use water than edible glue for this.

Airbrush cleaning jar and **cleaner** A glass jar used to safely contain the spray when you clear your airbrush to empty it of colour. Airbrush cleaner is a liquid that helps remove colour from inside. It is used like the colour itself, dropped into the colour well.

Cutters The cutters I use are all food-grade metal. When pushed down on to icing, these give you a cleanly cut shape. Some are multi-part (like the shoe cutter), while others are single part.

Double-sided sticky tape This is used to secure ribbon around cake or boards.

Palette knife Used for tasks as diverse as mixing icing, filling piping bags, applying jam to sponge and moving delicate decorations.

Rice paper Also called edible paper or wafer paper, whatever you do with normal paper you can create with rice paper – but you can also eat it!

Bread knife A large serrated knife is used to carve the large cakes into shape before icing.

Stencils Food-grade plastic stencils are ideal to build up your confidence and make a perfect design every time.

Craft punches Craft punches can be used with rice paper to punch out different shapes; I have used the butterfly punch.

Scrap paper This is used to create masks and to test colours before using the airbrush on your cake.

Rolling pin I use three rolling pins: one large, for rolling out large amounts of fondant (surgarpaste) and marzipan; one medium-sized rolling pin for rolling out modelling paste, and one small for rolling out flower paste very thinly.

White fat This helps to stop fondant (sugarpaste) from sticking.

Veiners Sandwiching flower paste between the two pieces of a veiner will create a leaf with realistic-looking veins.

Edible lustre Edible lustre is designed to be dusted on either before or after airbrushing. It creates an attractive shimmery effect.

Non-stick board Cutting boards designed for food preparation, these are available in many colours. I prefer green because the colour can be seen through the paste when rolling it out very thinly. You then know the paste is the correct thickness for petals and other decorations to be cut out from it.

Anti-bacterial wipes Anti-bacterial wipes are useful to clean up any mess and to keep your knives clean.

Sponge Natural sponge can be used to texture icing and to apply airbrush colour directly to the surface.

Die cutter, dies and plates.

Die cutter Along with dies and plates, this machine is used to cut out intricate designs from rice paper.

Freezer bags Made airtight, these are perfect for keeping any unused icing fresh and minimising waste.

Dowelling rods These are used to support the weight of the cakes when they are stacked on top of each other.

Smoother A large flat plastic shape that helps you get your cake surfaces completely smooth.

Wire cutters These are used to trim wire flower stems to length.

Scissors General scissors are used for cutting out the ribbon and paper templates, while superfine scissors are used for tiny detailing.

Eggcup This is the perfect shape to support the shape of some sugar flowers while they are drying.

Cornflour dusting bag If your fondant (sugarpaste) is getting sticky, give it a gentle dusting of cornflour.

Tylose powder This is added to modelling paste to help it set harder.

Kitchen paper This is useful in general, but particularly handy when cleaning out your airbrush.

> **Tip**
> To clean and keep your non-stick board in good condition, massage it with a little white fat, then wipe it with kitchen paper.

TECHNIQUES

The following techniques show you how to get started with your airbrush and how to cover cakes. Do not be intimidated – while all airbrushes differ in detail, they all work in broadly the same way, so the basic techniques are identical whatever airbrush you have.

Setting up an airbrush

The very first thing you do is to get your airbrush hooked up the compressor and get the power going – then you are ready to go. Simple!

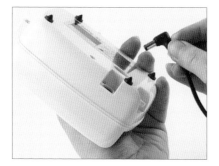

1 Attach the electric cable to the compressor.

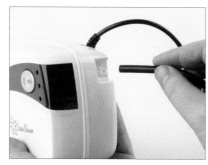

2 Attach one end of the hose to the compressor. Some airbrushes may require you to screw the hose in place; others (like the one I use in this example) simply require you to push it in place.

3 Attach the other end into the airbrush itself.

4 If your airbrush has a holder, clip it in place on the compressor. Turn on the power, and the airbrush is ready to use.

Adding and mixing colours

Airbrushes have a well of colour. Yours may be gravity-fed, like the one shown here, where you have an integrated cup into which you drop liquid colour. Do not overfill the colour well, as it becomes easy to spill. It is much better to simply refill it every so often with the mix you need. As a general rule, try not to add more than eight or so drops to the well at once.

Some airbrushes have a separate screw-on jar which you fill with colour, but the principles described below in mixing colours apply in the same way – you simply mix the colours in the jar before attaching it, rather than in the cup.

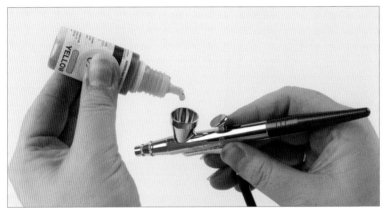

1 Squeeze the dropper bottle gently to deposit foodsafe colour drop by drop into your airbrush. Remember, do not overfill the colour well.

2 Turn your compressor on, and turn it to a low pressure setting (this may be with a button, or a knob). Hold the airbrush like a pen, and gently pull back the lever to spray the colour onto a piece of scrap paper.

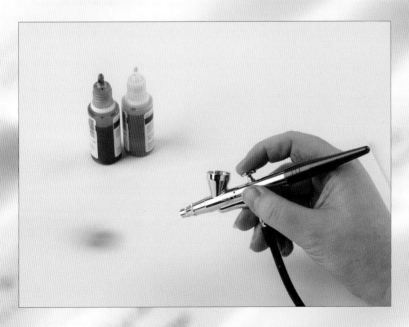

3 You can mix any hue by adding different colours into the well together. Here I have added some blue drops into the well filled with yellow to make a green. Always add the lighter colour first.

Cleaning your airbrush

Cleaning the airbrush after use is very important as you need to keep your airbrush in good condition. If any colour dries inside, you may find the lever feels floppy when you next use it. If this is the case, remove the airbrush from the hose and soak the airbrush in boiling water to dissolve the colour, then clean as described below. Be careful with the boiling water, as the airbrush will heat up.

1 Use up any spare colour in the well by spraying the airbrush into a cleaning jar. If you do not have one, spray it into an enclosed space – a plastic bag with kitchen paper at the bottom is good, as this absorbs the colour and prevents it bouncing up into the air. Depress the lever until the airbrush runs dry.

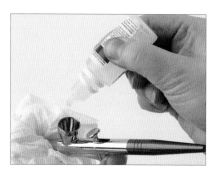

2 Hold a piece of kitchen paper to the end of the airbrush to plug the nozzle, and then add five or six drops of airbrush cleaner to the colour well.

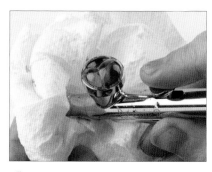

3 Holding the kitchen paper in place, pull the lever. This will force the air and cleaning fluid out of the joints. You will see the liquid bubble inside the colour well.

4 Release the lever, wipe off the airbrush with the kitchen paper, then wad up the end and gently wipe out the colour well. Repeat until no more colour comes out.

Airbrush hints and tips

Familiarise yourself with your airbrush before going any further. The diagram below shows the important parts of the airbrush I am using. Yours may differ, so make sure you can identify all the parts listed on yours before you continue with the instructions in the rest of the book.

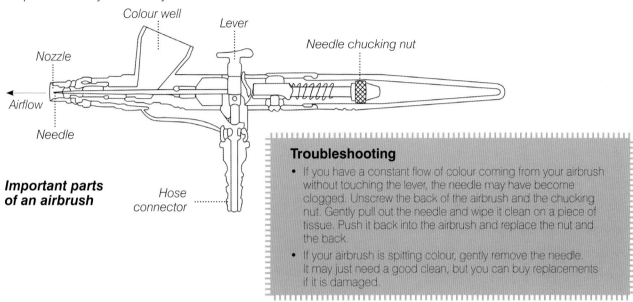

Colour well

Lever

Needle chucking nut

Nozzle

Airflow

Needle

Important parts of an airbrush

Hose connector

Troubleshooting

- If you have a constant flow of colour coming from your airbrush without touching the lever, the needle may have become clogged. Unscrew the back of the airbrush and the chucking nut. Gently pull out the needle and wipe it clean on a piece of tissue. Push it back into the airbrush and replace the nut and the back.

- If your airbrush is spitting colour, gently remove the needle. It may just need a good clean, but you can buy replacements if it is damaged.

Making a colour chart

Now you have set up your airbrush and know how to mix colours (see page 15), you are ready to have some fun using it. It is important to spend a little time mixing the colours to create a colour chart like mine, shown below.

Begin by filling your well with different proportions of the colours you have – for example, '3 drops of red to 1 drop of brown' and spraying it onto a piece of paper. Once dry, make a note on the piece of paper, cut out a small sample and stick it to a larger sheet. On my colour chart, I have grouped similar colour mixes – this makes it easy for me to quickly find a particular mix.

As well as being a great way to help build your confidence, having a colour chart to refer to will make it easy to match colours. For example, when you have a wedding cake to colour, you can match any swatches of ribbon to a mix on your chart.

Useful colour mixes

To get you started with your colour chart, here are some mixes I use a lot.

- 7 drops of yellow to 1 drop of brown will give you a lovely sunflower yellow.

- 5 drops of green to 4 drops of brown will make a more natural leafy green.

- 10 yellow drops to 1 brown will create a lovely cream colour when sprayed lightly.

- 7 drops of blue to 1 drop of black create a navy blue.

Lines

This technique is great fun and will help you build up your confidence in drawing the fine – and not so fine – lines that are a useful part of decorating using an airbrush.

Keep an eye on how the line differs depending on how far from the surface you spray.

The distance you hold the nozzle from the surface will make a difference to the result; as will the amount you pull the lever back. To build up your confidence start by making thin lines, then move on to thicker lines, as this will demonstrate these two vital points.

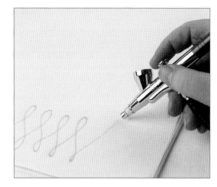

1 Add colour to the well and hold the airbrush like a pen. Holding the tip close to, but not on, the surface, very gently draw back the lever and draw the airbrush smoothly across the surface, as though using an ink pen. This will give you a fine line.

2 For thicker lines, hold the airbrush further away from the surface, and pull the lever back a bit further.

Tip

If you hold the airbrush too far away from the cake, the colour will float around the room instead of hitting the cake. Keep the nozzle no further than 12.5cm (5in) away from the surface of the cake.

Dots

Dots are another simple technique that help to show how the marks you make differ with distance. Some practice here will pay off later.

When adding dots, it is important that your airbrush nozzle is pointed directly at the surface, not at an angle. When spraying vertically, as shown here, it is especially important not to overfill the well or you risk spilling the colour out.

Tip

Once you know how to makes lines and dots, try drawing a little grid with lines, and practise adding dots where the lines cross to build up your confidence.

You can also try putting lines and dots together to create a music stave complete with notes!

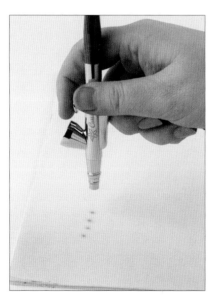

1 Add colour to the well and hold the airbrush almost vertically. Starting close to the surface, draw the lever back gently to create a dot. Be careful to release the lever completely before moving the brush, or you will end up with a little tadpole shape.

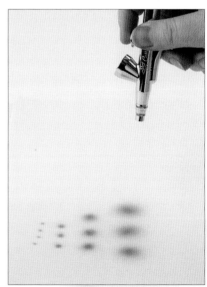

2 For larger dots, move the tip further from the paper, and pull back the lever further.

Using stencils

Stencils are a great tool that work especially well with airbrushing techniques. Always hold the airbrush directly opposite the stencil. If you hold it at an angle, the spray may go under the stencil and you will lose the sharp edge. Be careful not to overspray on top of the stencil as excess colour can end up under the stencil: we call this bleeding.

If the colour appears shiny, it is overwet and may smear or come off when you lift away the stencil from the surface.

Tip

Masks are temporary stencils made from scrap paper. They work in the same way – by shielding areas of the surface from the spray.

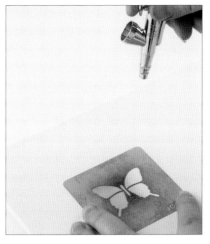

1 Lay the stencil in place and add colour to the well. For a solid fill, hold the brush directly overhead, approximately 7.5cm (3in) from the surface. Pull back the lever and move the airbrush in tiny circles to fill the area completely. Allow to dry before continuing.

2 Once dry – this will take just a few moments – carefully lift away the stencil to reveal a solid-coloured shape.

Tone and shading

Overspraying multiple light layers of the same colour over an area allows you to gradually build up the tone. The airbrush makes this so easy.

1 Lay the stencil down and hold the brush approximately 10cm (4in) from the surface, and spray a very fine, even layer, as described above.

2 Hold the airbrush closer to the surface and overspray the part of the image you want to strengthen or darken (in this case, the body of the butterfly stencil).

3 Allow to dry, then remove the stencil, to revel the subtle shading you have created.

Covering a cake

Most of the projects in this book are worked on cakes covered in fondant (sugarpaste), and these pages show you how to do it. To ensure best results, always cover the cake in marmalade, jam or jelly before covering the surface.

You will need

20cm (8in) fruit cake

1kg (2¼lb) marzipan

Icing sugar to stop sticking

1kg (2¼lb) white fondant (sugarpaste)

Jam/jelly or marmalade

25.5cm (10in) drum board

Palette knife

Turntable

Large rolling pin

Smoother

Kitchen knife

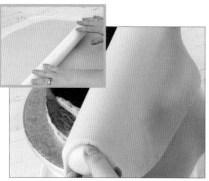

1 Place a drum board on your turntable, then put the cake on top, upside-down so that the top is flat. Fill the space between the cake board and the cake with marzipan as shown. Fill any small holes with marzipan as well, in order to create as smooth a surface as possible. Use small pieces of marzipan around any parts of the top edge that are angular, in order to help create an even curve all round. Boil your marmalade or jam (traditionally apricot jam is used), then allow to cool before smoothing a very thin layer all over the surface using a palette knife.

2 Warm up your marzipan by kneading it, and roll it out to a size large enough to cover the whole cake, with some spare. Roll it to an even thickness of 4mm (¼in). Lift the marzipan up and over the cake, using the rolling pin to support it, and drape it over the cake.

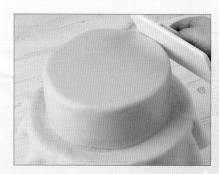

3 Roll over the top of the cake to drape the marzipan as evenly as you can. Draw out the excess with your hand, then use the edge of your palm to push in the edge, to flatten the marzipan onto the side of the cake without creases.

4 Using a smoother with one flat edge, smooth the top of the cake with gentle pressure and large round motions. Smooth the edges, using the flat edge at the bottom to get a crisp shape, then use a rocking motion to create an even curve around the top edge.

5 Use a sharp knife to trim away the excess marzipan (see inset). Use a pastry brush to dampen the marzipan with boiled water that has been allowed to cool.

6 Warm your fondant (sugarpaste) icing by kneading it, then roll it out to the same thickness as the marzipan.

7 Drape the icing over the cake. Smooth the top in the same way as the marzipan, easing out any air bubbles by lifting the icing at the edge and smoothing the bubble out towards the edge.

8 Use a smoother to smooth the sides and edge in exactly the same way as the marzipan.

9 Cut away the excess icing with a sharp knife, then use the ball of your thumb and the palm of your hand to gently polish the edge of the cake as shown.

10 Prepare any other cakes that the project requires in the same way. When stacking them, lift them off the board with a knife. You can use ribbons to cover the gaps, as shown. Never leave a cake on an unprepared board, as the moisture of the cake can make it appear mouldy. Instead, lift it off and place it on a drum board iced in the same way as the cake.

Tip
You can check roughly how much marzipan or fondant (sugarpaste) you need to roll out by holding your rolling pin up to the cake, and using this as a measuring stick.

Using royal icing

Royal icing is a sweet, slightly runny paste used for neatening the edges of the cakes, gluing tiered cakes together, fixing decorative items in position and for piping decorative patterns. It is so versatile! I use it for most of my cakes.

You can thicken the consistency of the paste by adding more icing sugar. You can keep home-made royal icing in the refrigerator for up to two days, but it must be covered and will need re-beating before use.

You will need

500g (1lb) icing sugar
70ml (2.5fl oz) made-up
Meri-white or pasteurised
dried egg whites
Two drops of lemon juice
Large bowl
Electric whisk or spoon
Greaseproof paper

1 Put the icing and egg together in a mixing bowl and mix together.

2 Continue mixing until the icing forms soft peaks as shown.

3 Cut a 20cm (8in) strip of greaseproof paper, fold the corner over to the opposite edge, then use a sharp knife to cut along the long edge.

4 Curl one of the sharper corners (i.e. one with a more acute angle) over into the centre to form a cone.

5 Holding the cone in shape, wrap the other corner round the back and up to the top.

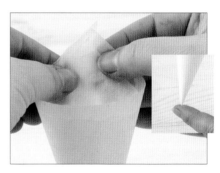

6 Line up the three corners at the top opening as shown. This will tighten the tip of the cone to a fine point (see inset).

7 Fold the lined-up corners down to keep the piping bag in shape.

8 Fill the bag by spooning the icing inside.

9 Fold the top edges over until you begin squeezing the icing down.

10 Fold the corners in at the top, then fold the end over.

11 Use a pair of scissors to cut the very tip off, and squeeze the bag to release the icing.

Tip

Meri-white or pasteurised dried egg whites should be used rather than fresh egg to minimise the risk of salmonella. To make up dried egg white, follow the pack instructions, then leave the dried whites to stand in the water for about thirty minutes in the refrigerator before use, otherwise the mix will be lumpy. The mixture can be strained to remove any lumps before adding to the icing sugar.

Piping bags and buttercream

You can also use steps 3–11 above to create larger bags for piping buttercream, or simply use store-bought disposable piping bags, as shown here.

Buttercream is less sticky than royal icing, so you can use a palette knife to fill the bag.

SUNSET SILHOUETTE

This project will teach you how to graduate colours to create a stunning sunset effect. It will also show you how to use stencils to airbrush simple silhouettes on the side and a focal image on a plaque on top. While intended as an engagement cake, the same principles apply to any similar design.

1 Set one fruit cake on top of the other, with marzipan in between to stabilise them, then cover with fondant (sugarpaste) icing as described on pages 20–21. Cover the drum board with fondant (sugarpaste) and place the cake on top. Put the board and cake on top of your turntable, then run a small amount of fondant (sugarpaste) around the gap, and use the smoother to hide the seam.

2 Knead a thumb-sized piece of modelling paste into a circle. Wet the back of it lightly with a waterbrush, then place it on the side of the cake where you wish the sun to sit.

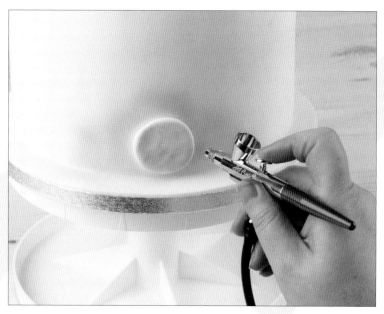

3 Set up the airbrush and add six drops of yellow to the colour well. Test the colour on a piece of scrap paper, then colour over the sun in a rough semi-circle, holding the airbrush 5cm (2in) or so away from the cake.

4 Work around the sides of the cake in the same way, aiming for even coverage. Move the airbrush slowly from side to side, and turn the turntable rather than moving your arm to cover the sides.

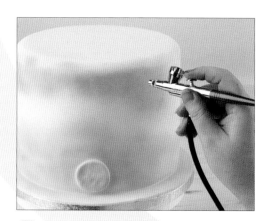

5 Without cleaning the airbrush, add two drops of red to the colour well and spray the top of the cake. Hold the airbrush the same 5cm (2in) away from the cake, and leave a white gap between the yellow area and the new area. Move the airbrush to work round the sides of the cake.

6 Add eight drops of yellow and one red to make a burnt orange. Check the colour on a spare piece of paper. Fill the white gap with the orange mix, working slightly over the other areas to create a smooth blend.

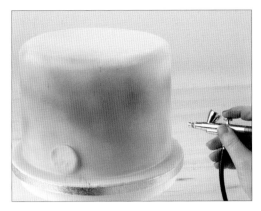

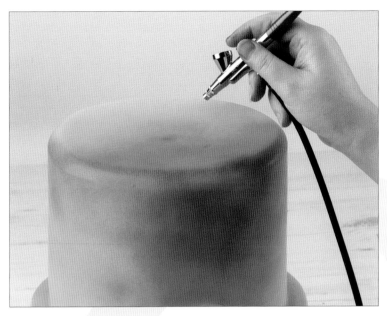

7 Turn the turntable to continue covering the sides in the same way. Top up the colour well with the same mix of eight drops of yellow and one red if you start to run low.

8 Use the same mix and method to cover the back and the top of the cake. When spraying the top, hold the brush a bit further back – roughly 15cm (6in) – to avoid any inadvertent lines.

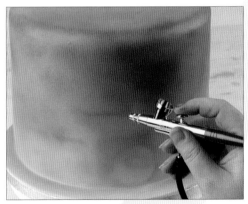

10 Add eight drops of yellow and one of red and, holding the brush close to the cake, draw some subtle horizontal lines to add some interest to the sky.

9 Carefully remove the modelling paste to reveal the sun, then spray over the area using one or two drops of yellow.

11 Referring to page 94 for the templates, create paper masks by using a craft knife to cut out the shapes of the figures, the lamp-post and the tree from scrap paper. Keep them at the bottom of the paper as shown.

12 Empty the airbrush in the cleaning jar, then add three drops of black to the colour well. Hold the mask against the cake, with the figures silhouetted in front of the sun. Working one shape at a time, spray the shapes while gently holding the mask in place. Masks work just like stencils, as described on page 19.

13 Dip a fine paintbrush in the black colour remaining in the well (see inset), and use it to add finer detail like branches and leaves on the tree.

The finished image on the cake at this point.

14 Roll out some modelling paste to 3mm (1/8in) thick, and use a sharp knife to cut out a heart shape roughly 9cm (3½in) across. Place the heart on a piece of foam to dry overnight.

15 Lay the stencil over the top and use the airbrush to spray black over the top.

16 Remove the stencil, then make a ball from a piece of modelling paste. Flatten one edge slightly.

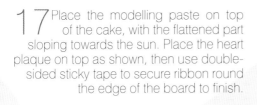

17 Place the modelling paste on top of the cake, with the flattened part sloping towards the sun. Place the heart plaque on top as shown, then use double-sided sticky tape to secure ribbon round the edge of the board to finish.

SHOE CELEBRATION

Create a fabulous life-size shoe to sit on top of your cake and learn how to airbrush leather effects and animal prints to really set it off. We will also be creating a realistic scarf with a fabulous animal print. You will be surprised how quickly this cake comes together – the hardest bit is waiting for the shoe to dry. Perfect for a birthday party, the recipient can keep the shoe once the cake has been eaten!

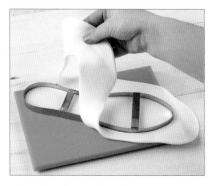

1 Rub a little white fat on your hands, then knead a block of modelling paste to warm it slightly. Roll it out to a thickness of 0.5cm (¼in). Lift the modelling paste away from your board, then replace it. This helps stop it sticking to the board when you cut out the shape.

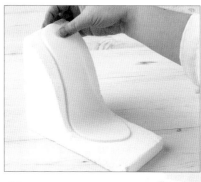

2 Use the shoe cutter to cut out the sole. Carefully lift it away and place it on the former, with the heel aligned with the top rear edge.

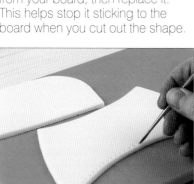

3 Roll out more modelling paste and cut out the toe strap and back pieces of the shoe in the same way. Use a small spoon-ended modelling tool to add the suggestion of stitch marks around the edges.

4 Use a waterbrush to wet the inner sides of the toe strap piece and place it on top of the sole in a curve as shown, sticking the wet parts to the sides of the sole. Make sure the stitching is on the outside. Use a scrunched-up piece of kitchen paper to help support the shape as it dries.

5 Wet the inside edges of the back piece and secure it in place as shown. Leave the shoe to dry.

6 Take a piece of modelling paste the size of your palm – approximately 100g (3½oz) – and add a teaspoon of Tylose powder to it. This helps strengthen it.

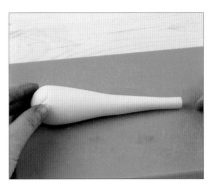

7 Knead the Tylose powder into the modelling paste and roll it into a tapered shape a little like a carrot.

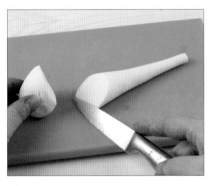

8 Use a sharp knife to cut it to 12.5cm (5in) long, with the broad end at an angle as shown. This will be the heel.

9 Place the heel on a piece of foam as shown, and leave to dry.

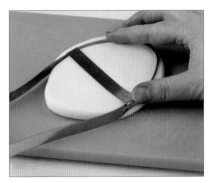

10 Roll out a piece of modelling paste to a 1cm (½in) thickness and use the toe end of the shoe cutter to cut out a wedge.

11 Wet the top flat surface with a waterbrush, place the shoe on top, and cut away the excess with a sharp knife to create a wedge under the toes.

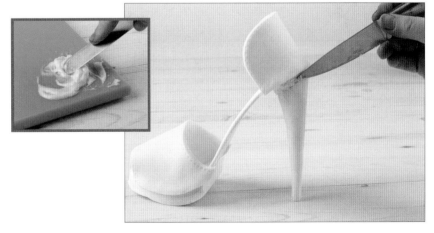

12 Add plenty of water to some modelling paste, and work it in with a palette knife until it takes on a chewing gum-like consistency (see inset). Use this as a glue to secure the heel to the sole of the shoe. Smooth the join with the flat of a knife. Look at the heel from different angles to make sure it is straight, then set it aside to dry.

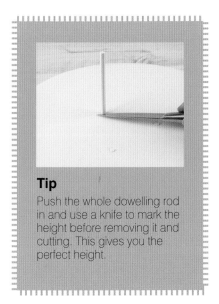

13 Hide the join by wrapping a 1.5cm (¾in) strip of modelling paste around the top of the heel, trimming away any excess. Put the shoe to one side to dry overnight.

14 Cover the 35.5cm (14in) drum boards with fondant (sugarpaste) as described on pages 20–21. Cover the 30.5cm (12in) cake with fondant (sugapaste), place it on top of the board and hide the join with some extra fondant (sugarpaste). Add the supporting dowelling rods to the centre of the cake.

Tip
Push the whole dowelling rod in and use a knife to mark the height before removing it and cutting. This gives you the perfect height.

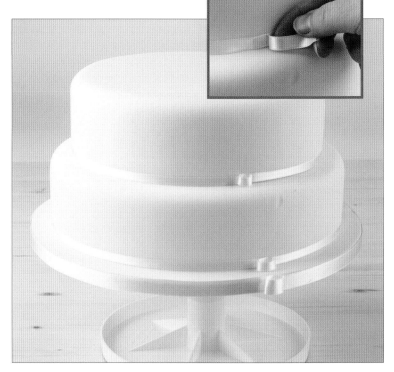

15 Place the 25.5cm (10in) cake on the thin board and cover with fondant in the same way. Use a large palette knife to lift the iced cake onto the top of the larger cake.

16 Run white ribbon round the drum board edge, and around the bottom of each cake. To secure ribbon on the cake, add a touch of double-sided sticky tape on one end of the ribbon, wrap it round the whole cake, and attach the other end. Add a touch of double-sided sticky tape on the tail end of the ribbon and turn it back on itself to form an attractive end (see inset).

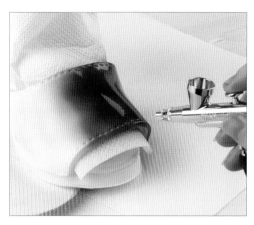

18 Using a piece of kitchen paper to protect the sole, spray the toe strap with brown. Work closely and quite heavily, until you see a distinct shine. This heavy use will create a lovely leather effect.

17 You may wish to put some kitchen paper down to protect your surface. Paint the sole of the shoe with the airbrush, filling the colour well with a cream mix of ten drops of yellow and one of brown. Be sure to colour the sides of the soles, too.

19 Spray the wedge below the toe strap in the same way. Aim the airbrush carefully to avoid hitting the sole.

20 Colour the back of the shoe in the same way, using the kitchen paper to help protect the sole, then spray the inside, working carefully to avoid the sole. Set the shoe aside to dry.

21 Rub some white fat on your hands, then knead a block of modelling paste to warm it slightly. Roll it out to a thickness of 2mm (1/16in) in a long thin strip. Hold it up to the cake to check the length. It should drape all the way from the bottom to the top and back down.

22 Lay it back down flat, then use a sharp knife to trim the sides flat. Using a cream mix of ten yellow to one brown, colour the whole piece with the airbrush. Work very lightly.

23 Change to pure brown and add a random series of rough dots.

24 Turn the piece over and fold the outer edges in to hide the sides. Next, turn it back over and fold it like a concertina (see inset), then drape the piece over the cake, with a loose loop slightly off-centre. Secure the piece in place using a waterbrush.

25 Use a small paintbrush and brown colour to add small loops around the dots.

26 Repeat over the whole scarf to finish the animal print design.

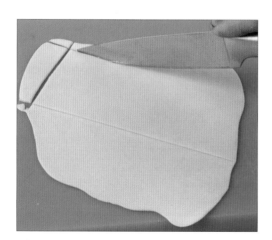

27 Roll out a small piece of fondant (sugarpaste) icing very thinly and cut it into a 4 x 6cm (1½ x 2½in) rectangular panel.

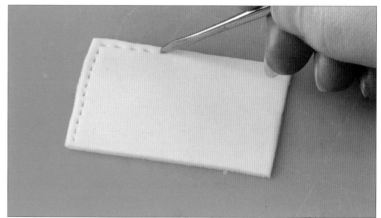

28 Use a small spoon-ended modelling tool to add the suggestion of stitch marks around the edges.

29 Use a waterbrush to attach the small rectangular plaque in place on the shoe as a label.

30 Make a 2.5 x 4cm (1 x 1½in) panel from modelling paste, decorate it with the leopardskin pattern (see steps 22–26) and secure it in place on the foot of the shoe using royal icing.

31 Add a 23cm (9in) length of diamanté trim around the top of the wedge and a 11.5cm (4½in) length around the top of the heel, securing them in place with royal icing.

Tip
Diamanté trim is not edible, so do let the recipient know when you present the cake.

32 Place the completed shoe in position on the top of the cake. If you leave it unattached, the recipient can keep the shoe once the cake is eaten.

Tip
You can personalise your shoe by painting a message such as 'Happy Birthday' or the recipient's name onto the label of the shoe.

MOON CAKE

You can really let your imagination go with this one! I love space and want to show you how to create the wonderful impression of planetary systems using the airbrush. There are lots of different textures and effects you can give planets, from fine rings and weather systems to the suggestion of deep three-dimensional craters made by overspraying water droplets.

You will need

Two 15cm (6in) fruit cakes
2.5kg (5½lb) marzipan
2.5kg (5½lb) white fondant (sugarpaste)
20cm (8in) and 25.5cm (10in) square drum boards
Airbrush and cleaning jar
Turntable
Large palette knife
Small kitchen knife
Circular cutters: 2.5cm (1in), 3cm (1¼in), 5cm (2in) and 7cm (2¾in)
100g (¼lb) modelling paste
Waterbrush
Liquid food colour: blue, orange, yellow and black
Natural sponge
Pointed-ended modelling tool
1m (39in) of 15mm (½in) thick dark blue ribbon
Double-sided sticky tape

1 Use double-sided sticky tape to stick the smaller drum board on top of the larger one, in the centre. Cover the drum boards with fondant (sugarpaste) icing as described on pages 20–21. The only difference here is that there will be excess icing at the corners, so work especially carefully here.

2 Set one cake on top of the other, with marzipan in between to stabilise them, then cover with fondant (sugarpaste) icing in the same way. Use a large palette knife to lift the iced cake away from the board on which it was iced and onto the top of the prepared boards. Use a small amount of fondant to fill in the gap between cake and boards, then use the back of the knife to smooth the area over.

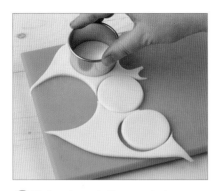

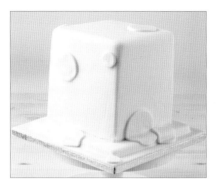

3 Roll out modelling paste to a thickness of 2mm (1/16in), then use circle cutters to cut out four 2.5cm (1in), two 3cm (1¼in), six 5cm (2in) and one 7cm (2¾in) circles.

4 Dot these over the surfaces of the cakes and board, securing them temporarily with a little water from a waterbrush. Where they fall over corners, be careful not to pull the circles out of shape. Feel free to overlap one or two.

5 Set up the airbrush and add ten drops of blue to the colour well. Test the colour on a piece of scrap paper, then add random hazy lines and streaks over every side and the top.

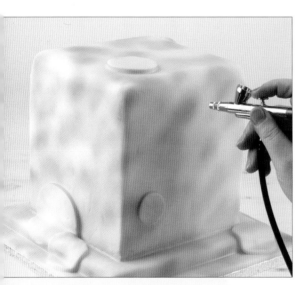

6 Build the colour up gradually with multiple thin layers rather than with a single heavy spray. Refill where necessary.

7 Add five blue drops and one black drop to the colour well to make a navy mix, and use this to repeat the process. Work in random loose lines and streaks again, covering some of the underlayer and some of the white still showing.

8 The modelling paste circles will block the paint, so work in from different angles to make sure you catch all the sides. This helps to ensure crisp edges later on.

9 Continue building up the colour, using pure blue to colour in any remaining white areas. Make sure you have worked over the whole cake and the iced drum boards.

10 Add a gentle haze of pure black, holding the airbrush further back than before. This is to darken the overall colours without covering all your work.

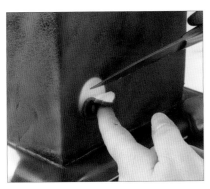

11 Clean your airbrush while the cake dries thoroughly, then use a sharp knife to carefully lift away the modelling paste circles to leave blank planets in space.

12 Load the airbrush with pure blue. Squeeze the waterbrush over one of the planets on the iced board to add one or two droplets of water to it. To add craters on vertical edges (i.e. the sides of the boards), use a paintbrush to paint on clean water in a small circle.

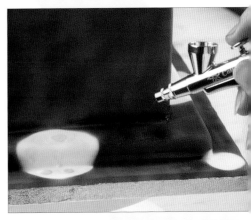

13 Hold the brush 10cm (4in) away from the planet, and very lightly draw back the lever to spray the planet without moving the water droplets.

14 Clean the brush and load it with orange. Very lightly add shading to the large planet by colouring just the left-hand side and bottom edges as shown. Leave a fine light edge showing.

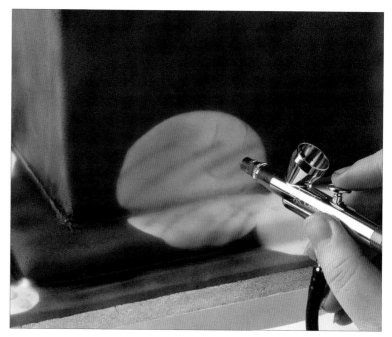

15 Strengthen the colour evenly across the whole planet to leave one side in shade, then add very fine lines that follow the curve of the planet.

16 Make a shading mix of five drops of blue and one of black, and gently strengthen the shaded area with a broad hazy line.

17 Shade the other planets in the same way. You can add details by drawing fine lines as rings round the planets, or by dabbing the colour on directly using a natural sponge, as shown here.

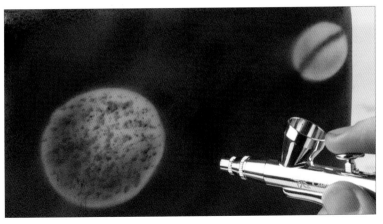

18 You can soften in the sponging and ring effects with more colour or shading.

19 Finish colouring the planets in the ways described above, using the colours and techniques you like best. Add the suggestion of tiny stars across the cake with the pointed end of a modelling tool, by gently scraping the colour to reveal the clean white icing beneath.

20 Add a few larger stars in the same way, but scraping it into a flared cross, as shown. Be careful not to dig too deep or you risk revealing the cake. No matter the size of the design, it needs to stay shallow enough to reveal only the white surface of the icing.

21 For larger effects, like this exploding asteroid, scrape out a small central area, then use the edge of a palette knife to guide the tip of the modelling tool. Add a larger spot on the end furthest from the centre.

22 To finish, secure a dark blue ribbon round the edge of the board using double-sided sticky tape.

SPIRIT OF NATURE

My dad was a farmer and I grew up loving the great outdoors. Making this wise old tree stump will teach you how to airbrush textured surfaces. You could add little fairies and much more to personalise this fun cake, ideal for a quirky birthday celebration.

You will need

Two 20cm (8in) round fruit cakes

38cm (15in) drum board

1.5kg (3lb) marzipan

2.5kg (5½lb) white fondant (sugarpaste)

800g (1¾lb) modelling paste

Airbrush and cleaning jar

Liquid food colour: brown, black, blue, yellow, red, green

Sharp-edged modelling tool

Craft knife

Small rolling pin

Small amount of royal icing in a piping bag

Tea strainer

Waterbrush

Cutters: grass

3m (118in) of 15mm (½in) thick cream ribbon

Double-sided sticky tape

1 Place one 20.5cm (8in) cake on top of the other, and cover with marzipan, as explained on pages 20–21. Place the cakes on top of a 38cm (15in) drum board, slightly off-centre.

2 Make a teardrop shape out of modelling paste, then pinch the bottom to make a simple nose. Secure it to the marzipan using a waterbrush.

3 Add two little loops of modelling paste on either side of the nose for eye sockets.

4 Fill the eye sockets and add a mouth with smaller amounts of modelling paste.

5 Still using modelling paste and the waterbrush, add some roots around the cake.

6 Working in sections, build up an uneven 'crown' around the top of the cake with modelling paste.

7 Roll out your fondant (sugarpaste) icing and cover the whole cake and the drum board. Use the sharp edge of a modelling tool to add lines all round the tree stump to give the texture of wood. Work over the whole wooden area, including the inside of the crown. Avoid the flat top of the cake within the crown, leaving this smooth.

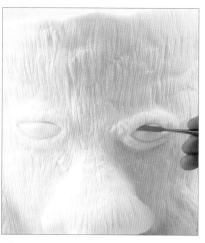

8 Carefully press round the underlying modelling paste to bring out the features, then use the modelling tool to bring out the shape of the eyes.

9 Place the cake on top of the turntable. Set up your airbrush and fill the well with brown. Working in up-and-down motions to follow the woodgrain, and no more than 5cm (2in) from the surface, colour the trunk of the stump. Work slowly and carefully, making sure to work into the surface texture and get an even colour all round the roots. Refill the well as necessary.

10 Turning the turntable, work round the whole stump until you come to the features. Work particularly carefully around the eyes. Bring the airbrush in very close to the eyelids and angle the brush to avoid the eyes themselves.

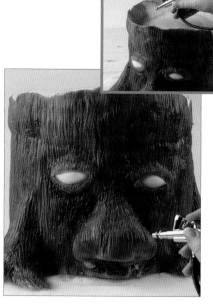

11 Work into all the nooks and crannies of the nose, and finish covering the wooden area. Paint the textured inside of the crown (see inset) in the same way.

12 Using the same brown colour, but pulling the airbrush back for a softer effect and lighter tint, paint the smooth inside of the trunk. Hold the airbrush nearly vertical and use slow circular movements.

13 Still using brown, use the fine lines techniques (see page 18) to draw a thin spiral line outwards from the centre of the smooth inside.

14 Using the sharp edge of a modelling tool, scratch a few fine lines radiating outwards from the centre of the spiral to add texture.

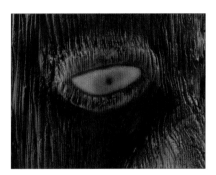

15 Clean your airbrush. Next, fill the well with blue and draw two large dots in the middle of the eye.

16 Clean the airbrush again, then add a pupil to the centre of each eye with a very fine dot of black.

17 Add a soft haze to the whites of the eyes using a small amount of the brown. This softens the white of the eyes and stops them being too stark.

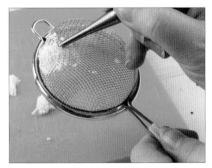

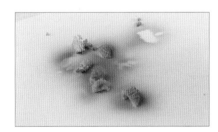

18 Clean the airbrush, then add five drops of green and four brown to the colour well. Use this earthy-green mix to colour the board. Work in small, slightly uneven circular motions to create a natural, slightly uneven, finish.

19 Put the cake to one side to dry. Push some modelling paste through a sieve to create a mossy effect. Use a small rolling pin or other tool to gently scrape small pieces off. Place them down on a cutting board.

20 Move the pieces onto a piece of scrap paper and use the airbrush to spray them green. These pieces are small, so work from a little way away to avoid blowing them straight off the paper. However, you also need to spray them from all angles in order to work into the recesses. Once coloured, put them to one side.

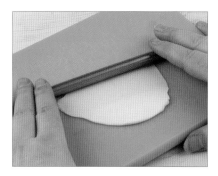

21 To make the tufts of grass, use the small rolling pin to roll out small pieces of modelling paste, so that one side is thinner than the other.

22 Use the grass cutter to cut out a grass shape, making sure the flat edge is on the thicker part of the paste, and the ends of the grass on the thinner part.

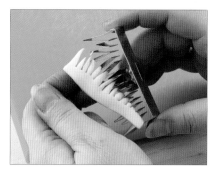

23 Lift away the cutter, and push the thicker end of the shape out. Carefully peel the rest of the paste out of the cutter.

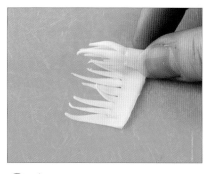

24 Use a waterbrush to wet the bottom edge, then roll up the base of the grass tuft, with the wet part inside.

25 Stand the tuft upright and squeeze the base from all sides so that the ends fan out.

26 Make half a dozen grass tufts in the same way and place them to one side to dry.

27 Shape a piece of modelling paste into the shape of half a flat mushroom cap, then use a small knife to score the underside in a radiating pattern to represent the gills.

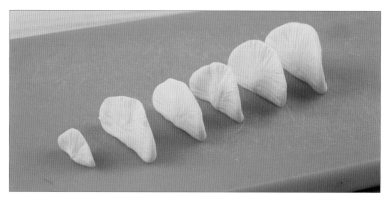

28 Make half a dozen in different sizes, then set them aside to dry.

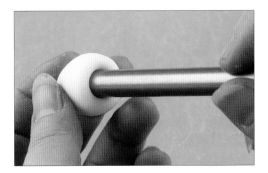

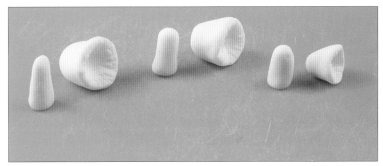

29 Push the end of your small rolling pin into a small ball of modelling paste and shape it into a bell-shaped mushroom cap.

30 Make another two or three, then make stalks for each from a small rod of modelling paste. Score the insides of the caps using a craft knife, then set all of the parts to one side to dry.

31 Once all the pieces are dry, use the airbrush to colour the grass tufts with the earthy green mix (five drops of green and four brown); the tops of the flat mushroom caps with yellow and the bottoms with one part brown to nine parts yellow; the tops of the bell-shaped mushroom caps with red and the bottoms with brown; and the mushroom stalks with very pale brown – simply spray them with brown but from further away.

32 Use royal icing to assemble the bell-shaped mushrooms, then attach them to the woodland floor along with the grass tufts. Still using royal icing, attach the flat mushrooms to the tree stump himself along with some of the moss. Attach the remaining moss across the cake as you wish.

33 To finish, run cream ribbon round the rim of the drum board, securing it with double-sided sticky tape.

ROCK 'N' ROLL FLAMES

Flames are a versatile design that are so easy to achieve with an airbrush. I have kept them simple on this cake, but you could layer them up or use different colours for an even more striking effect.

You will need

Two 18cm (7in) round sponge cakes

25.5cm (10in) drum boards

2.5kg (5½lb) white fondant (sugarpaste)

450g (1lb) buttercream

Scrap paper

Scissors and glue stick

Airbrush and cleaning jar

Liquid food colour: red, yellow and black

250g (½lb) modelling paste

Guitar cutter

Small amount of royal icing in a piping bag

1m (39in) of 15mm (½in) thick red ribbon

Double-sided sticky tape

1 Stack one 7in (18cm) sponge on top of the other, securing them with buttercream. Place the cakes on a 25.5cm (10in) drum board, then cover with marzipan and fondant (sugarpaste) icing as described on pages 20–21. Use a smoother to smooth the edges.

2 Trace the large mask template on page 95 on to a piece of scrap paper and use scissors to cut out the large mask.

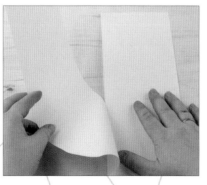

3 Fold a second piece of paper in half lengthways and tear it in two.

4 Use a glue stick to attach the end of the strip of paper to the top of the large mask.

50

5 Continue adding strips until you can closely wrap the entire cake with the mask and the strip. Glue the pieces at the other end to secure.

6 Move the mask up and down until the flames sit at the correct height on the cake. You will be able to see the top of the cake through the paper.

7 Use the small mask template on page 95 to cut out some individual smaller flame shapes from spare scrap paper.

 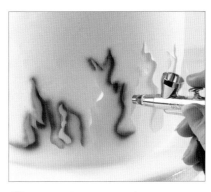 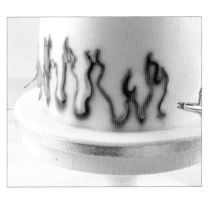

8 Set up your airbrush and add red to the colour well. Starting at one end of the large mask, hold the airbrush close to the cake and draw a fine line on the edge of the mask, following the shape of the flames. Aim to keep the line of colour half on and half off the edge of the mask, as this will give the crisp edge.

9 Work in long, smooth movements to trace the edge of the flames. Do not worry about holding the mask in position, as the pressure of the air will press the mask down as long as you work from straight on.

10 Continue working round to the other end of the mask.

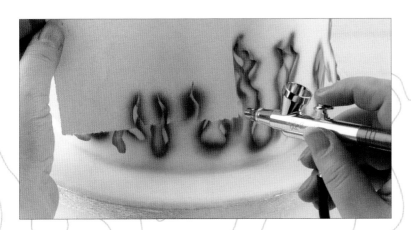

11 Still using the red in the airbrush, hold up the small mask and add a few small flame marks within the larger flame area. Be careful to use only the top end of the flames – if you work too far down towards the edge, you'll get an ugly straight edge.

12 Turn the small mask round and use it to add some details on the iced drum board.

13 Once dry, carefully lift away the large mask to check the effect on this section.

14 Without cleaning the airbrush, add yellow to the colour well and carefully work over the flame area. Work fairly closely and straight onto the surface to give you control.

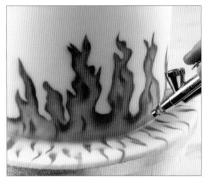

15 Pulling away slightly to get a more diffuse effect, spray yellow over the drum board, working outwards from the base of the cake.

16 Add red to the colour well – again without cleaning it – and overspray the drum board, again working outwards from the base of the cake to create a smooth blended graduation of colour.

17 To finish the section, add subtle blending strokes of red to the small internal flames using short flicking motions from the base of the individual flame upwards. This completes one section of the flames

18 Allow the colour to dry, then place the large mask back on the cake, further round the edge.

19 Using the large and small masks, colour the rest of the edge and cake board rim, as described above.

20 Use the template on page 95 to make the top mask. Place it on the top of the cake, then begin to colour round the edge in the same way as for the sides of the cake. Again, use red in the colour well.

21 Unlike the large mask, you hold the top mask in your hand. This allows you to move it round and select different flames, giving a more random effect. Make sure all the flames come outwards from the centre towards the edge.

22 Work all the way round the top, then change to the small mask. Use this to add some smaller flames within the area. As with the top mask, make sure the small flames all point outwards from the centre.

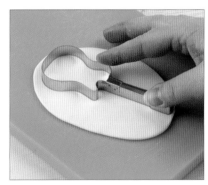

24 Roll some modelling paste out to a thickness of 5mm (¼in), and use the guitar cutter to cut out at least three guitar shapes.

Tip

Modelling paste decorations like this can be fragile, so you might like to cut out a spare or two, in case of breakage before the big day.

23 Without using any masks, add some soft filling to the area with any remaining red in the well. Add yellow to continue filling in the area, using movements that work out from the centre to the edges. Move the cake to one side.

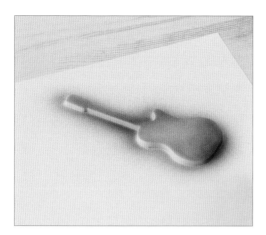

25 Place one of the guitar shapes on a piece of foam and allow to dry thoroughly. Clean your airbrush, add black to the colour well and lay a grey layer over the top and sides of the guitar.

26 Build up the colour to a solid flat black with two or three repeated layers. The reason for this is that black works best when built up gradually for a smooth effect.

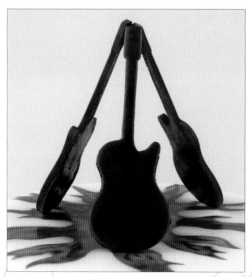

27 Make three guitars in total, colouring the backs when the fronts are thoroughly dry. Use royal icing to secure the three guitars in place on top of the cake, with the heads touching.

28 To finish, secure red ribbon round the edge of the drum board using double-sided sticky tape.

DAY OF THE DEAD

As well as learning how to carve this shape – perfect for a Hallowe'en party or simply a spooky birthday – out of a sponge cake, this project will also teach you shading and fine airbrushing techniques, as well as making use of the 'scary trees' technique (see page 11) to make cracks in the skull.

You will need

Three 23cm (9in) sponge cakes

31cm (12in) drum board

Fondant- (sugarpaste) covered 31cm (12in) drum board

Turntable

450g (1lb) buttercream

1kg (2½lb) white fondant (sugarpaste)

Large bread knife

Teaspoon

Palette knife

Airbrush and cleaning jar

Liquid food colour: black, yellow, green, brown, teal, pink, violet, blue, orange

1m (39in) of 15mm (½in) thick cream ribbon

Double-sided sticky tape

1 Working on a 31cm (12in) drum board, layer three 23cm (9in) sponge cakes on top of one another, securing them with buttercream, to give a cake with a height of at least 16.5cm (6½in).

2 Use a bread knife to carve the cake in a curve, taking approximately 4.5cm (1¾in) off each side to leave the base of the cake as a rough oval, 23cm (9in) long and 16.5cm (6½in) across.

3 Begin to carve the back of the skull, using the bread knife to create a curve down to the bottom as shown.

4 Carve a wedge of the cake away on the opposite side at an angle to create the front of the skull. The cake should have the rough shape of a motorcycle helmet at this point.

5 Turn the cake so the front faces you, then carve away a little on either side to suggest the cheeks. The remaining surface of the cake (visible as the darker area) will form the chin.

6 Round off the sharp edges to refine the basic shape of the head, then use the back of a teaspoon to push in a small hole in the centre of the front; roughly halfway between the chin and the top. This is the nose recess.

7 Spoon out eye sockets on either side of the nose, in line with the top of the nose recess.

8 Using the eyes and nose as reference points, carefully carve away cake to create the cheekbones, temples and jawline.

Tip

If you have time, leave your carved cakes in the fridge overnight before covering. Then they will accept buttercream more readily and crumble less.

9 Carefully adjust the shape by trimming away small amounts of cake and shaping it with your hands and fingertips.

10 Place the drum board on top of the turntable. Use a palette knife to cover the whole skull with buttercream, then carefully brush away any excess crumbs.

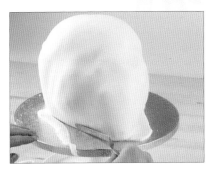

11 Roll out a large amount of fondant (sugarpaste) icing and drape it over the skull.

12 Use the edge of your hand to tuck the icing in around the jawline and at the back of the skull.

13 Use a palette knife to trim away the majority of the excess, leaving a border at the base of the cake. Use the edge of the palette knife to tuck the icing under the cake.

14 Use your hands to smooth the surface, then gently rub the features to bring out the eyes and nose.

15 Continue shaping the fondant (sugarpaste) icing round the skull with your fingers, working into the temples, jawbone and cheekbones.

16 Set up your airbrush and add five yellow drops and one brown to the colour well. Use this to give the whole cake a subtle layer of a bone colour.

  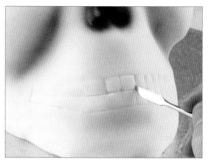

17 Clean the airbrush and add three drops of brown and one drop of black into the colour well. Use small circular motions to gradually build up the colour in the eye sockets and nose recess. Work carefully and slowly and keep the pressure on the lever light.

18 Build up a softer tone in the temples and cheekbone hollows by spraying from slightly further away. Continue being gentle when working the lever.

19 Use the edge of a modelling tool to carve the teeth. Start by making three parallel horizontal lines, then add a vertical line to join them in the centre. From here, add vertical lines to either side then round off the squares on the centre line to give a more realistic edge to the teeth.

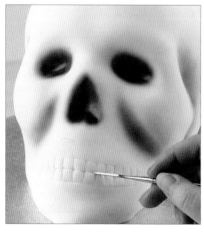 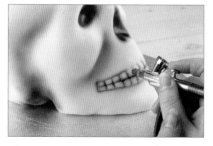 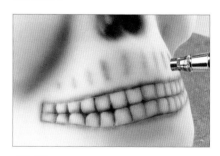

20 Finish carving the teeth.

21 Using the airbrush and the same dark brown mix of three brown drops and one brown drop, shade the mouth. Work extremely carefully between the individual teeth, barely pulling back the lever and working with the tip of the airbrush close to the cake.

22 Working a little further back, but with the same gentle touch, add some subtle lines above the teeth.

23 To add cracks (I am adding one on the back), hold the airbrush right next to the surface and spray until a small pool of liquid is formed.

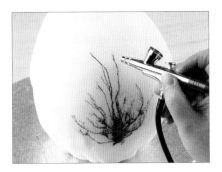

24 Release the trigger and chase the pool of liquid out to form long cracks.

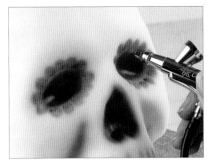

25 Clean the airbrush and add pink to the well. Use this to add petals around the eye sockets and a line around the nose recess. Again, work carefully and gradually, with the nozzle of the airbrush close to the surface of the cake.

26 Clean the airbrush, then outline the nose using red.

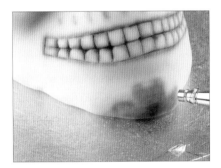

27 Cleaning the airbrush between each colour, add a teal flower on the chin, building it up with small circular motions, before drawing a slightly stronger outline with the same colour.

Tip
You might like to think of the primrose shape as four hearts with the points touching in the centre.

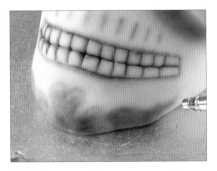

28 Add green leaves on either side of the flower on the chin.

29 Clean the airbrush and fill the well with black. Add a small dot at the top of the cheekbone.

30 Starting from the dot, draw a fine tapering line across under the eye that ends near the top of the nose recess.

31 Add three small dots beneath the first one, and draw another tapering line that runs from the bottom dot to the end of the first line. Add some decorative flourishes if you wish.

32 Decorate under the other eye in the same way, then add a similar shape above each eye.

33 Using the dots you added earlier to guide your fine lines, join up the shapes around the eyes with cobweb-style decoration.

Tip

If your airbrush will not produce a very fine line, then you can use a fine paintbrush to paint on any of these lines, or even use an edible pen.

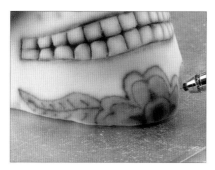

34 Starting from the outside borders and working inwards, outline the leaves and flower on the chin. Add a large dot of black in the centre of the flower.

35 Using the needle, add further decorations and details like dots and outlines around the face.

36 Continue decorating the skull as you wish. I have added some further flowers with purple and yellow, plus orange and black dots and flourishes. Finally, transfer the cake to an iced drum board and run cream ribbon around the edge, securing it with double-sided sticky tape.

CREAM TEA

Airbrushing is fantastic for subtle colouring effects. This project will show you how to make a topsy-turvy tea party, where all the scones are actually sponge cakes in disguise! They are quick to create, delicious and look stunning. When creating the scones try to make them look lumpy, not smooth like we traditionally make cakes.

You will need

Eight 6cm (2¼in) cupcakes

500g (1lb) white fondant (sugarpaste)

500g (1lb) buttercream

Strawberry jam

Bread knife and cutting board

Airbrush and cleaning jar

Liquid food colour: brown, yellow

Disposable piping bag and large star nozzle

Scissors

Tea strainer

Icing sugar

Teaspoon

Craft knife and cutting mat

Palette knife

Scrap paper

1 Use a bread knife to cut each of your cupcakes in half, then roll out fondant (sugarpaste) icing to a thickness of 2mm (1/16in), and place one half of the cupcake in the middle. Allow plenty of space around the cake.

2 Use a craft knife to cut a large circle around the cupcake half, making sure there is enough icing to fold up around the sides.

3 Remove the cupcake half, check the fondant (sugarpaste) icing is not sticking to the surface, then spread a thin layer of buttercream over the circle of icing using a small palette knife.

4 Replace the cupcake half and start to fold the fondant (sugarpaste) icing up around the edges. This can be a bit messy, so you may find it easier to cup the cupcake in your hand.

5 Cut away excess fondant (sugarpaste) icing and crimp it round as shown.

6 Turn the cupcake half over, but do not smooth the icing. Use your fingers to shape it into the form of the bottom half of a scone, with a few lumps and bumps.

7 Repeat the steps above with the other half of the cupcake, to make the top half of the scone.

8 Set up your airbrush and add nine drops of yellow and one brown to the colour well. Place the top of the scone on a piece of scrap paper. Holding the airbrush 7.5cm (3in) away from the top of the scone, gently pull back on the lever to dust it with a little colour.

9 Colour the bottom of the scone in the same way. When colouring the top of the bottom half, you can avoid spraying the cake if you wish, but there is no need to do so. Work right down to the bottom edges.

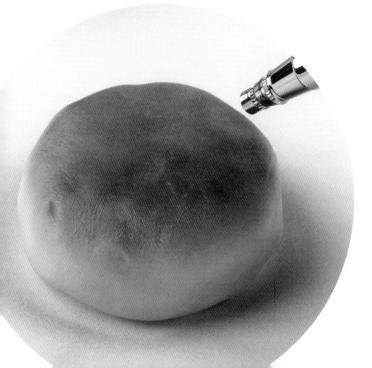

10 Empty the airbrush and add brown to the colour well. Holding the airbrush slightly closer to the top of the cake, use small circular motions to add the suggestion of a well-baked top.

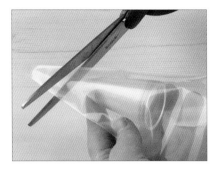

11 While the paint dries, take a disposable piping bag and slip the star-shaped nozzle inside, then use a pair of scissors to trim the end of the bag to the right length for the nozzle.

12 Push the nozzle up so that the end is clear of the bag, then use a palette knife to fill the bag with buttercream.

13 Twist the end of the bag round and squeeze the buttercream to the end of the nozzle, then begin piping the buttercream onto the bottom half of the scone.

14 Work round the edge, then into the middle to cover the surface with piped buttercream.

15 Use a teaspoon to add some strawberry jam on top of the buttercream.

16 Place the top of the scone on top of the bottom half, then use the end of a palette knife to dress the jam a little bit, encouraging it to drip artistically over the cream.

17 Use a tea strainer to dust the top with a little icing sugar to finish the scone.

18 Make as many more as you need. To add a little variety, arrange one or two in pieces, with the jam and buttercream showing.

BUTTERFLY CELEBRATION

This elegant cake has a cinched-in waist to suggest the bodice of a wedding dress, a tapering strip of delicate butterflies to evoke happiness and joy, and a beautiful bouquet of cream chocolate roses, delicately kissed with the airbrush to add a pink blush to the edges of the petals.

You will need

One 28cm (11in), two 25.5cm (10in), and two 20cm (8in) fruit cakes

Two 35.5cm (14in) drum boards, one pre-iced

4.5kg (10lb) marzipan

4.5kg (10lb) white fondant (sugarpaste)

Bread knife

Palette knife

Jam/jelly

Smoother

Rice paper

Airbrush and cleaning jar

Liquid food colour: pink

Large butterfly punch

Fine paintbrush

Royal icing in a small piping bag

Craft knife

1kg (2½lb) white chocolate modelling paste

Freezer bags

1m (39in) of 15mm (½in) thick white ribbon

Double-sided sticky tape

Cornflour

1 Working on a 35.5cm (14in) drum board, stack the following fruit cakes in order: a 28cm (11in) cake on the bottom, a 25.5cm (10in) cake on top of that, then two 20cm (8in) cakes, and finally a 25.5cm (10in) cake on top. This will give a tiered cake with a height of at least 38cm (15in). Fill the larger gaps with marzipan, then use a bread knife to carve the cakes into a smooth curve as shown.

2 Continue working round the cake, carefully carving it into a tapered curve all the way round. Next, use a palette knife to cover the cake with cooled boiled jam or marmalade, as usual when covering a cake.

66

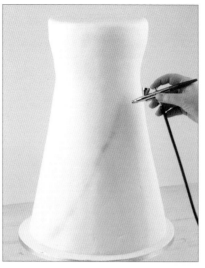

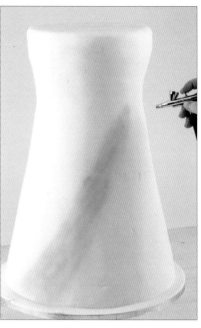

3 Roll out a large sheet of marzipan and cover the cakes as described on pages 20–21. The crucial difference when laying the sheet of marzipan on is that you work almost sideways, covering the side of the cakes rather than draping it down from the top. Use a smoother to smooth it in place, as usual (see inset). You will probably have to add a little extra marzipan to help cover the top.

4 Ice the cake in the same way, smoothing it down. Place the cake on an iced 35.5cm (14in) drum board and then on to a turntable. Set up your airbrush and add pink to the colour well. Starting from the base of the cake, work a smooth curved line up to the 'waist' (the thinnest part of the cake). Start working around 10cm (4in) away from the surface, to give yourself a faint guideline.

5 Broaden the line a little, but keep the colour fine and diffuse. Set the cake to one side.

6 Still using pink in the airbrush, lightly spray a sheet of rice paper. Use smooth side-to-side motions and keep the nozzle a uniform 7.5cm (3in) away from the surface to give a flat, smooth finish.

7 Put the prepared rice paper in a large butterfly punch and press the punch down (see inset). Remove the resulting rice butterfly from the punch.

8 Clean and turn off the airbrush, add black to the colour well, and use this as a palette to paint the border of the butterfly with a fine paintbrush. Use light feathery strokes of the brush to give a soft edge.

9 Add some further details on the butterfly (as shown above). Make fifty in total, and put two to one side for later. Take one of the remaining butterflies and make a fold on either side of the butterfly's body so the wings look in flight.

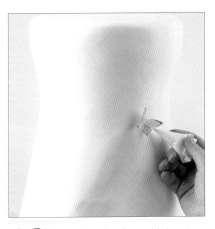

10 Use a touch of royal icing to attach the body at the end of the sprayed area, near the waist.

11 Cut the next butterfly in half using a craft knife. Add a little royal icing to the back of one half.

12 Attach it to the outside of the pink line, just behind the first butterfly.

13 Use royal icing to attach the other half of the butterfly on the other side of the line.

14 Cut more butterflies in half and attach on either side of the pink line right down to the bottom, then return to the top and attach more butterfly halves to overlap the previous layer.

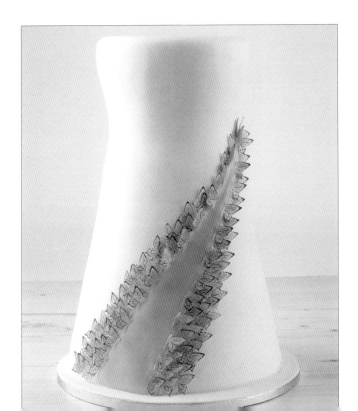

15 Continue building up the effect by adding touches of royal icing to the backs of the butterfly halves and slipping them behind the previous row. Add more rows at the bottom to give a thicker effect. Aim to reinforce the curve of the original airbrushed stripe.

16 Put the cake to one side, dust a board with cornflour, and make a 2.5cm (1in) tall cone from white modelling chocolate.

17 Dust the inside of a freezer bag (or other clear plastic bag) with cornflour and place a 1.5cm (¾in) ball of white modelling chocolate just inside the mouth.

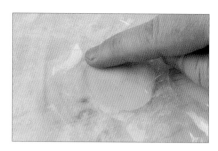

18 Press the other side of the bag down to squash the ball, then work round the edge of one half to create a thin edge. This will be one petal.

19 Secure the thicker end round the base of the cone, leaving the thin edge free and extending a little way past the point of the cone.

20 Wrap one side round to form a sharp point at the top.

21 Wrap the other side round, leaving a small gap at the top as shown.

22 Make another petal as before, and attach on the other side (where the edges of the previous petal sit). Make sure the top of the petal sits at the same height as the first. Wrap it slightly more loosely than the first.

23 Make and wrap a third petal in the same way, starting a third of the way round from the previous petal.

24 Add a fourth and fifth petal, each a further third round, and wrap them more loosely. Gently curl these petals outwards.

25 Continue adding petals round the outside to complete one rose. I find around nine petals in total gives a good effect.

26 Set up your airbrush and add pink to the colour well. Bring the nozzle close to the rose and add a very faint tinge to the very edges of the petals.

27 Slightly reinforce the points of the petals (where they begin to curve outwards) to finish the colouring.

28 Use a palette knife to carefully cut away excess chocolate in order to give the rose a flat base.

29 Add a small dome of fondant (sugarpaste) to the centre of the top of the cake, securing it with water, then use a palette knife to place the rose on the edge of the dome.

30 Make nine more roses in the same way, and arrange five of them on the same level as the first, around the dome. Next, add a smaller dome on top of the first dome and arrange the remaining flowers round the top.

31 Use a touch of royal icing to attach the two remaining butterflies on top.

32 Using pink in the colour well, gently overlay colour to strengthen the pink stripe, working slightly over the edge of the butterflies to blend them in.

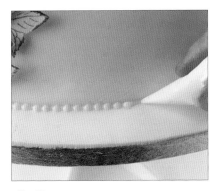

33 Use a piping bag of royal icing to add beads between the cake and the board. Work smoothly round the board, drawing the icing from left to right, and regularly pushing backwards on the line to create little beads.

34 To finish, secure a white ribbon round the rim of the drum board with double-sided sticky tape.

HARVEST

A pumpkin is a useful shape to know how to carve. It is ideal for Hallowe'en, but can also make a beautiful centrepiece for a harvest festival celebration. The airbrush makes adding realistic shading and colouring a breeze, but my favourite part of this project, which takes me back to my roots carving flowers from vegetables, is carefully carving away the surface colour to reveal a beautiful pattern in the underlying white fondant (sugarpaste). I have included a diagram for a floral pattern for you to use if you like (see page 94), but you should feel free to carve any design you choose.

(see page 94)

You will need

Three 23cm (9in) round sponge cakes
31cm (12in) drum board
2.5kg (5½lb) fondant (sugarpaste)
450g (1lb) buttercream
Jam/jelly
Large bread knife
Turntable
Palette knife
Large rolling pin
Smoother
Point-ended, angled sharp-ended and spoon-ended modelling tools
Small amount of royal icing in a piping bag
Airbrush and cleaning jar
Liquid food colour: yellow, red, brown and green
1m (39in) of 15mm (½in) thick cream ribbon
Double-sided sticky tape

1 Stack the three 23cm (9in) sponge cakes on top of one another, applying layers of buttercream with a palette knife between them to secure the layers together.

2 Use a large bread knife to carve the cakes into a smooth curve from the top to the bottom all the way round.

3 Carve a cross into the top of the cake using the bread knife.

4 Carve a second cross at forty-five degrees from the first to make an eight-pointed star, then use this to guide you in carving eight recesses all round the cake, resulting in a pumpkin shape.

5 Soften any hard edges with the knife, then scoop out a little hole at the top for the stalk to sit in.

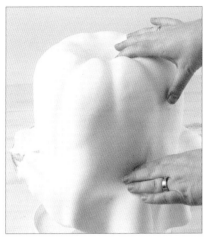

6 Cover the cake with jam/ jelly, then knead the fondant (sugarpaste) icing and drape it over the shaped cake. Start to ease it gently into the shaping.

7 Tuck the excess underneath, being careful to avoid any creases, then trim away any that still remains.

8 Using the smoother, smooth the surface of the cake, working into the curves and recesses.

Tip

Be careful when adding jam to your carved sponge because it can make the cakes slip around when icing them.

9 This smoothing may cause the shaping of the cake to look a bit angular, so gently reinstate the curves in the creases and hollows using your fingers.

10 Set up your airbrush and add seven drops of yellow and one of red to the colour well for an orange mix. Test the colour on a piece of scrap paper, Working in a smooth up-and-down motion, begin to colour the pumpkin. This movement helps to get into the dips and recesses, but also suggests the natural lines of growth on a real pumpkin.

11 Using the turntable to rotate the cake, continue to colour the pumpkin until it is completely orange. Never stop in the middle of a stroke, even if the paint runs out, as this causes blotches. Instead, wait until you are at the top or the bottom of the movement to release the lever, then add more of the same mix (seven drops of yellow and one red drop) to the colour well.

12 Using the same orange mix, begin to strengthen the colour in the recesses and the hollow at the top with an overlaid layer.

13 Using flicking motions, and working from the top downwards, work down the sides to overlay and strengthen the colour.

14 Add some shading at the bottom of the pumpkin, again by overlaying the same mix.

15 Add some variation in the recesses with very light strokes of pure brown to give a dusting. This will also knock back some of the vibrancy of the redder parts and make the pumpkin appear more natural.

16 Still using light dusting strokes of brown, deepen the shading at the bottom, particularly in the dips.

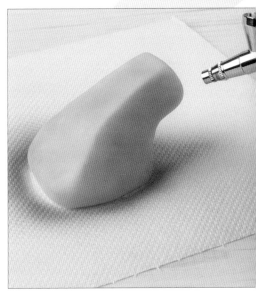

17 Take a 5cm (2in) diameter ball of modelling paste. Squeeze the middle and one end gently into a roughly four-sided shape.

18 Put the other end on your surface and tip the narrowed end over, then elongate it to form a pumpkin stem.

19 Add two drops of green and two of brown to the colour well to make an earthy green. Use this to colour the stem.

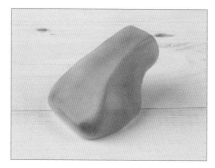

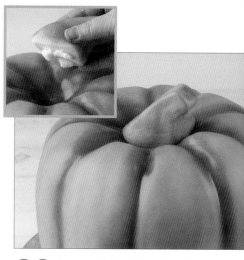

20 Avoiding the corner edges of the stem, lightly spray it with pure brown; including the very end.

21 Add one or two drops of green to the colour well and overlay the stem with a light spray, again avoiding the corner edges.

22 Use royal icing (see inset) to secure the stalk in place in the central recess of the pumpkin.

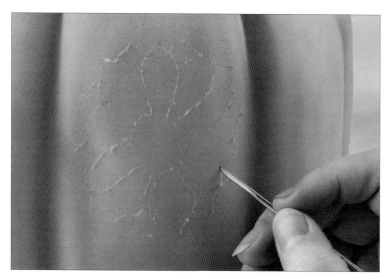

23 Using the fine-pointed end of a modelling tool, start to lightly etch the outline of the central flower in the middle of one of the bulging areas of the pumpkin. Refer to the diagram on page 94. Keep your marks very faint, barely removing the paint.

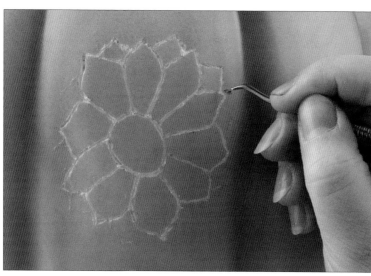

24 Using the angled sharp end of a modelling tool, begin scraping 1mm (1/32in) or so into the surface so the white icing becomes visible following the initial lines. As a guideline, work from the outermost points towards the centre; but ignore this if it is uncomfortable – work however best suits you and the design. Lightly brush away any excess colour.

25 For fine details like the veins of the leaves and the texture on the flower centre, use the fine pointed end of a modelling tool. Flare the line of the veins out towards the centre, and use tiny circling marks for the flower centre itself.

26 For larger areas, lightly mark the outline with the end of a spoon-ended modelling tool.

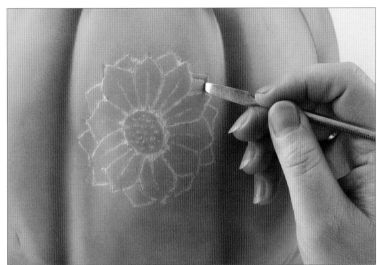

27 Lift away the shape with the flat end of a modelling tool. Be very careful not to work too deeply – you are aiming simply to reveal the icing beneath the colour. If you dig too deeply, you will reveal the cake!

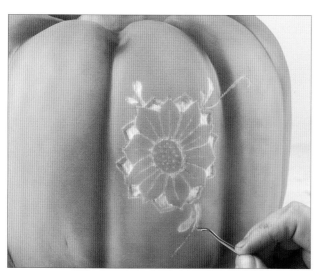

28 With the pointed, spoon and flat ends of the tools, you can work the design outwards from the centre. Work gradually and step back every so often to check the design is fitting correctly.

29 With the design complete, transfer the cake to a drum board covered with fondant (sugarpaste) icing. Use double-sided sticky tape to secure cream ribbon round the edge of the board to finish.

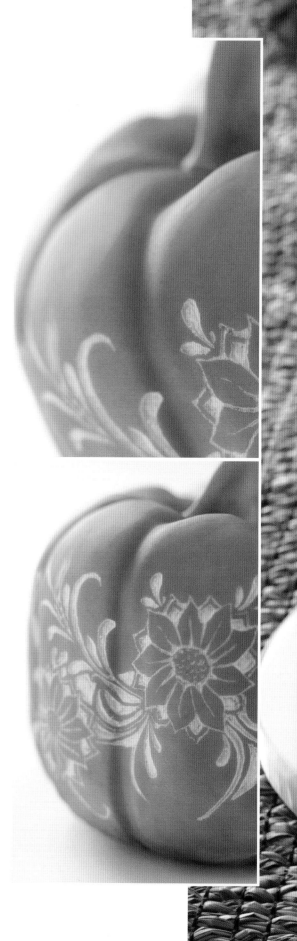

BRIDAL BOUQUET

Traditionally a bride's bouquet is laid beside the cake. Here, it's part of it! I have a passion for sugar flowers – they were the first things I ever made from sugar when I was a child. These orchids and sea holly, along with a mix of variegated ivy leaves, will make any plain white iced cake look amazing.

You will need

15cm (6in), 20cm (8in), 25.5cm (10in) fruit cakes

3kg (6½lb) marzipan

3kg (6½lb) fondant (sugarpaste)

Ten dowelling rods

Flower paste

White fat

Thin rolling pin

Non-stick green board

Egg cup

22, 26 and 28 gauge white food safe wire

Wire cutters

Waterbrush

Tweezers

Fine (size 1) and 12mm (½in) flat paintbrushes

Airbrush and cleaning jar

Tea light

Liquid food colour: red, pink, yellow, brown, black, blue, and green

Pencil and scrap paper

Edible lustre: pearlised white shimmer

Half-width florists' tape: brown, green

Superfine scissors

Cutters: multi-part phalaenopsis orchid, sea holly, and three sizes of ivy leaf

Veiners: ivy leaf, multi leaf

Posy pick

3m (118in) of 15mm (½in) thick white ribbon

1 Rub a little white fat on your hands, then knead a piece of flower paste the size of your little finger to warm it slightly. Roll it into a sausage shape, then flatten it slightly using your fingers.

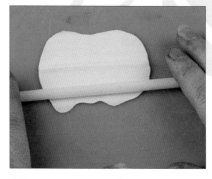

2 Put the small rolling pin in the centre of the sausage and press down, then roll it away from you. Lift the rolling pin away, replace it below the halfway mark, and roll towards you, leaving a slight ridge in the centre.

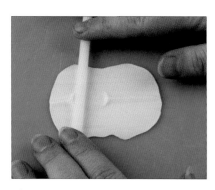

3 Leaving the ridge 3cm (1¼in) long, roll the flower paste out to the left.

4 Pick up the flower paste from the ridge end and lift it away to check it is not sticking. Replace it on the board, then use the small rolling pin to make it thin enough that you start to see the colour of the board beneath.

5 Place the orchid throat cutter over the flower paste, with the ridge in the centre of the stem as shown. Press down and wiggle it slightly to cut the shape.

6 Remove the excess flower paste. To ensure you do not end up with fluffy edges, run your finger round the cutting edge. This smooths the cut.

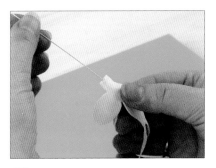

7 Use the wire cutters to cut an 18cm (7in) length of 28 gauge wire. Bend the end over to blunt it, then insert the blunt end into the thick part of the orchid throat formed by the ridge. Push it all the way to the end of the ridge.

8 Put the orchid throat in your hand (or on a piece of foam, if your hands are hot) and place the rounded end of the small rolling pin half on the edge of the flower, and half on your hand as shown. Run it round the edge of the rounded petals to create a realistic fine edge.

9 With the fine 'tongues' of the petal, run the rounded edge from the point into the centre to cause them to curl up.

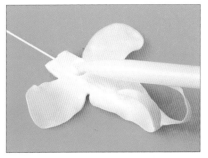

10 Roll a tiny ball of flower paste and press the pointed end of the rolling pin into the centre to create a dip. Pick up the ball (it should stick to the rolling pin) and place it in the centre of the orchid throat. Secure it in place with a little water from your waterbrush.

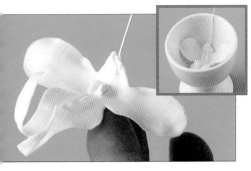

11 Pinch the base of the orchid throat around the stem, bend the wire as shown, then leave to dry in an egg cup (see inset).

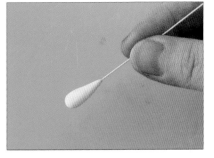

12 Use the wire cutters to cut an 18cm (7in) length of 28 gauge wire. Bend the end over to blunt it as before, then insert the blunt end into a small ball of flower paste and pinch the base to make a round-ended cone.

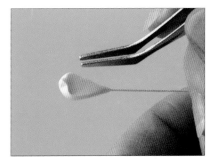

13 Use the round end of the small rolling pin to make a cup-shaped dip in the paste, then use tweezers to make a cut as shown. This completes the orchid centre.

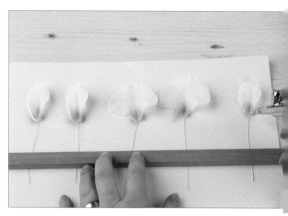

14 Cut out and wire the following petal pieces from flower paste: two 'arms', two 'legs', and a head. Use 12.5cm (5in) wire for each. There is no need to bend over the ends for these petals. When shaping the petals, remember they have a facing – one 'arm' will sit on the left, for example, and the other on the right, so they need to be shaped in the correct direction when arranged.

15 Set up your airbrush and add pink to the colour well. Use this to add a dot of colour to the base of each, near the wire. Do the same on the backs. If you hold them in place with a ruler or similar piece of wood, it makes things much quicker and easier. Colour both backs and fronts.

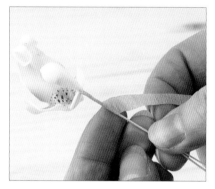

16 Use the airbrush to add a subtle touch of yellow to the centre of the throat, then add hints of red to both sides.

17 Using a small paintbrush and the red colour remaining in the airbrush well, add small dots and lines for detail in the throat.

18 Bend back the wire near the base of the throat piece, then place the orchid centre and secure it by wrapping the wires together with the light green half-width florists' tape.

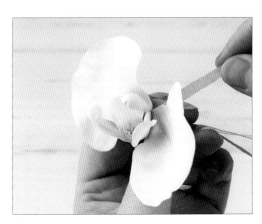

19 Add the 'arm' petals in place, bending the wires at the base and wrapping the florists' tape round once or twice.

20 Add the 'head' petal in the same way, then add the 'leg' petals. Wrap the florists' tape round all of the wires to create a firm but flexible stem and complete the orchid flower.

21 To make the orchid bud, put a small amount of flower paste on the end of a 18cm (7in) length of 22 gauge wire. Squeeze it into a roughly three-sided shape, then use the pointed end of the small rolling pin to score each side (see inset). Wrap the wire to complete the bud.

22 Make eight orchid flowers and seven buds in total. Secure three buds and four flowers together on a 35.5cm (14in) length of 22 gauge wire. Make a similar second stem with four buds and three flowers. Set the eighth flower to one side.

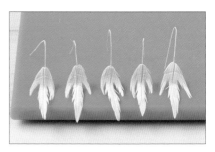

23 Following the instructions for the orchid throat earlier, roll out a small piece of flower paste leaving a ridge. Use the medium sea holly cutter to cut out the shape of the bract, leaving at least 2.5cm (1in) of ridge. Cut a 9cm (3½in) length of 28 gauge wire and insert it into the ridge.

24 Put the bract into a veiner, with the tip of the sea holly piece at the tip of the veiner. Press the other part of the veining piece down and lift away to add the texture.

25 Use superfine scissors to cut into the edges of the bract to add a feathered appearance, then bend the wire just below where the main part of the bract splits from the side pieces. Make four more sea holly bracts in the same way, then leave them all draped over the edge of your cutting board while you make the centre.

26 Bend the end of a 12.5cm (5in) length of 26 gauge wire over to blunten it. Prepare a pea-sized amount of flower paste. Light a small candle and hold the blunt end of the wire in the flame to heat it. Insert the hot end of the wire into the flower paste. This seals it firmly on the end.

27 Pinch the flower paste to give it a slightly pointed end, then use the superfine scissors to cut into it from the base upward. Work up to the point, snipping the flower paste into a spiky shape (see inset).

28 Add three drops of green and two drops of brown to the colour well and colour the parts of each bract past the bends. Colour both backs and fronts.

29 Use a navy mix of five drops of blue and one of black to colour the rest of the bracts and the centre. Work into the spiky centre from all angles, to ensure it is completely covered.

30 Wrap the wires of the pieces together using florists' tape, then use a 12mm (½in) soft flat brush to dust the central area with pearlised white edible lustre. Make two more sea holly flowers in the same way.

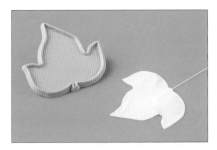

31 Following the instructions for the orchid throat above, roll out a small piece of flower paste leaving a ridge. Use the large ivy cutter to cut out the shape of the leaf, leaving at least 2.5cm (1in) of ridge. Cut a 10cm (4in) length of 28 gauge wire and insert it into the ridge.

32 Vein the piece in a large ivy veiner in the same way as the sea holly bracts, but aligning the bases rather than the tips.

33 Soften the edges as for the orchid petals, then pinch slightly where the flower paste meets the wire to create shape.

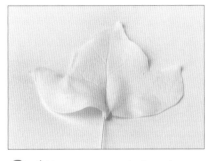

34 Use a cream mix (ten drops of yellow and one brown) to colour both sides of your ivy leaf.

35 Place the cutter you have used so the bottom is aligned with the edge of a piece of scrap paper and draw round it with a pencil, then draw a frilled shape inside the outline.

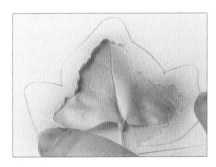

36 Lay the paper over the centre of the coloured leaf, and use it as a stencil to colour the ivy leaf with three drops of green and one of brown. Colour both back and front.

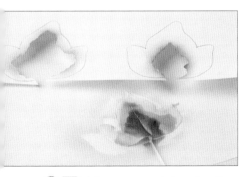

37 Make a second stencil, with a slightly smaller frilled shape, and use this as a stencil to spray the inside with a second layer of the same colour. Again, colour both back and front.

38 Use the appropriate cutters to make four large ivy leaves, seven medium ivy leaves and ten small ivy leaves in the same way. Use brown half-width florists' tape to wire them together into two groups, with the smaller leaves nearer the end, as shown in this example.

39 Wire all of the prepared pieces together, including the eighth flower you set aside earlier, into a pleasing arrangement.

40 Cover the cakes and drum board with fondant (sugarpaste) icing as described on pages 20–21. Stack the cakes, using supporting dowelling rods as described in steps 14–15 of the Shoe Celebration (see page 32). Put the cakes on the prepared board and use double-sided sticky tape to secure white ribbon round each join and the rim of the drum board.

41 Take the cake off the turntable. Put a posy pick on the end of the wire (never push unprotected wire into a cake) and push it firmly into the cake. You can now arrange the wired flowers and stems around the cake to show off the tiers.

Tip

Remember to remove the flower arrangement before cutting the cake, as the wire makes it non-edible. However, as it is made of sugar, it can be kept as a keepsake once the cake has been eaten.

CHRISTMAS SWIRLS

This Christmas cake is deceptively simple – the lace-like rice paper looks so delicate that people will think you have spent hours creating it. The swirling spiral lines and delicate decorations mean that it will brighten up any table. While intended as a Christmas centrepiece, it would also make a wonderful birthday cake for a child born in the winter months – give it a go!

You will need

31cm (12in) and 26cm (10in) drum boards

Two 20cm (8in) round fruit cakes

1½kg (3½lb) white fondant (sugarpaste)

1kg (2½lb) marzipan

Airbrush and cleaning jar

Liquid food colour: blue

Modelling paste

Die cutter and Wild Vine 588E Tonic Studios die

Small amount of royal icing in a piping bag

Snowflake stencil

Double-sided sticky tape

1m (39in) of 15mm (½in) thick white ribbon

1m (39in) of 15mm (½in) diamanté strip

Six sheets of rice paper

Cutters: 9cm (3½in) and 6cm (2¼in) circles

1 Set one fruit cake on top of the other, with marzipan in between to stabilise them, then cover with fondant (sugarpaste) icing as described on pages 20–21. Use double-sided sticky tape to stick the smaller drum board on top of the larger one, in the centre. Cover the drum boards with fondant (sugarpaste) and place the cake on top. Put the board and cake on top of your turntable, then run a small amount of fondant (sugarpaste) around the gap, and use the smoother to hide the seam.

2 Add pure blue to the colour well, then draw the airbrush quickly across the whole cake in a slow flicking motion to add light diagonal strokes.

3 Varying the distance you hold the airbrush from the surface, continue to add loose light strokes to the sides. Use the turntable to move the cake, rather than move the position of the airbrush. This helps to keep the stripes consistent all the way around the cake.

4 With the sides completed, begin to build up the top. Use diagonal strokes, but do not go all the way across the surface – instead, work from the point in front of you off to the right, turning the turntable.

5 Work round the whole of the top to create a spiral effect.

6 Strengthen the colour across the whole cake in the same way, if necessary. Put the cake to one side.

7 Roll out modelling paste to 4mm (¼in), then use a 9cm (3½in) circle cutter to cut a plaque from modelling paste. Roll out some more paste to 1cm (½in) thick and use a 6cm (2¼in) circle cutter to cut out a support. Leave these to dry.

8 Place all four parts of the Wild Vine die on the base plate (see inset). Lay rice paper over the top, then place the cutting plate on top.

9 Run the plates through the die cutter.

10 Remove the piece from the die and pick out the small internal parts, leaving the hollow shape shown. Make a second hollow ring in the same way.

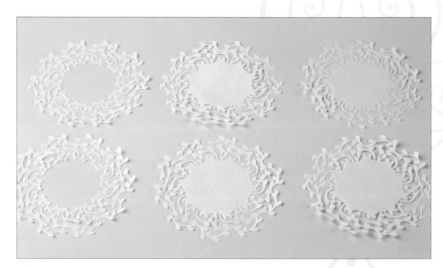

12 Place rice paper and then the cutting plate on top, and run through the die cutter to make a complete shape. Make four more complete shapes in total.

11 Take the two inner pieces of the die out.

13 Use the airbrush with blue and the snowflake stencil to add a snowflake design to the centre of each complete shape. Put all the rice paper to one side.

14 Use the airbrush to colour the plaque using blue and the same spiral technique used on the top of the cake.

15 Use dots of royal icing to attach the four complete rice paper shapes around the cake, spacing them evenly.

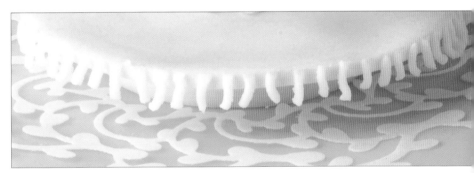

16 Use royal icing to secure one of the hollow rings on the top of the cake, then attach the support in the hole, again using royal icing.

17 Attach the plaque on top, again using royal icing, then decorate the edges using short lengths of royal icing.

18 Use modelling paste to make tiny snowballs. Build them up into a pile, using royal icing to secure them together.

19 Pick up the pile of snowballs on your palette knife and place the pile on top of the plaque, again securing with royal icing.

20 Use scissors to cut a quarter of the remaining hollow ring away.

21 Curl the ring around on itself, overlapping 2.5cm (1in) or so to make a partial cone. Secure the overlapping areas with royal icing, then place it over the snowballs.

22 To finish, run diamanté trim round the base of the cake, securing it with royal icing, then use double-sided sticky tape to attach white ribbon round the rim of the large drum board.

Tip

Diamanté trim is not edible, so remember to let the recipient know when you present the cake.

TEMPLATES AND DIAGRAMS

The templates on these pages are supplied at full size except where noted. Dotted lines indicate the bottom edge of the paper. Feel free to adapt the size and details of the reference diagram to suit the size of your cake and personal taste.

Template for the mask used for Sunset Silhouette on pages 24–29.

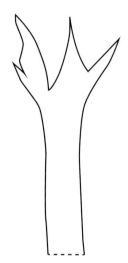

Reference diagram for Harvest on pages 72–79.

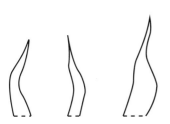

Template for the small mask used for Rock 'n' Roll Flames on pages 50–55.

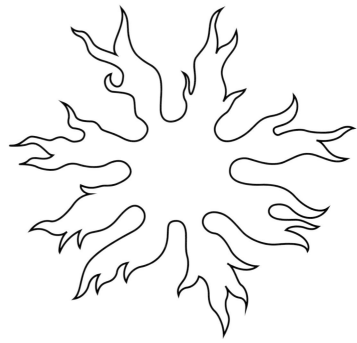

Template for the top mask used for Rock 'n' Roll Flames on pages 50–55, reproduced at half the actual size. You will need to photocopy it at 200 per cent for the correct size.

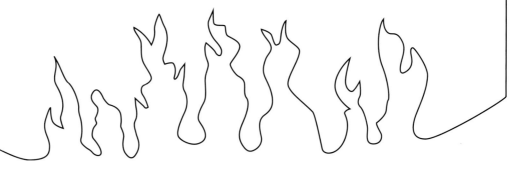

Template for the large mask used for Rock 'n' Roll Flames on pages 50–55, reproduced at half the actual size. You will need to photocopy it at 200 per cent for the correct size.

INDEX